LONDON
of one hundred years ago

JOHN COULTER

SUTTON PUBLISHING

First published in 1999 by
Sutton Publishing Limited · Phoenix Mill
Thrupp · Stroud · Gloucestershire · GL5 2BU

British Library Cataloguing in Publication Data
A catalogue record for this book is available from the British Library.

ISBN 0-7509-1886-1

The publisher gratefully acknowledges the assistance given by the Guildhall Library and the London Metropolitan Archives in the preparation of this book.

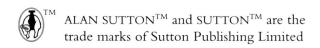
ALAN SUTTON™ and SUTTON™ are the
trade marks of Sutton Publishing Limited

Typeset in 11/13pt Bembo Mono.
Typesetting and origination by Sutton Publishing Limited.
Printed in Great Britain by WBC Ltd, Bridgend.

CONTENTS

ACKNOWLEDGEMENTS

My thanks to the staff at the London Metropolitan Archives, the National Monuments Record London Searchroom, and Westminster City Archives, to Christopher Lloyd and Malcolm Barr-Hamilton at Tower Hamlets Local History Library and Archives, and especially to Ralph Hyde, John Fisher, Jeremy Smith, and Lynne McNab at the Department of Prints and Maps, Guildhall Library, for their friendly help and learned advice.

I am also grateful to two old friends. Ken George kindly lent his charming postcard of Marie Lloyd. Richard Taylor volunteered his assistance at an early stage, and has contributed invaluably to every part of the book.

BIBLIOGRAPHY

The numbers after the entries refer to pages in *London of One Hundred Years Ago* on which illustrations from these books appear, or on which extracts from them commence. Names in brackets are those of quoted contributors to collaborative works.

Abbott, J.H.M., *An Outlander in England*, 1905; 13, 62, 83, 106, 112

Allingham, William, *Diary*, 1907; 7

Barbellion, W.N.P., *The Journal of a Disappointed Man*, 1919; 44, 67, 93, 99

Beerbohm, Max (ed.), *Herbert Beerbohm Tree*, 1920 (W.L. Courtney) 40

Besant, Sir Walter, *The Bell of St Paul's*, 1889; 28

Blunt, Wilfrid Scawen, *My Diaries*, 1919; 11, 23

Booth, Charles, *Life and Labour of the People in London*, 1902 (E.C. Grey) 3, 81, 99, 103, 107, 107, 117, 118

Builder, The 25

Butler, Samuel, *Alps and Sanctuaries*, 1882; 53

Collingwood, S.D., *The Life and Letters of Lewis Carroll*, 1898; 42

Cook, Mrs E.T, *Highways and Byways of London*, 1902; 5, 29, 31, 62, 65, 66, 69, 73, 80, 91, 103, 115, 121

Coulevain, Pierre de [Augustine Favre de Coulevain], *The Unknown Isle*, French ed. 1906, transl. 1911; 8, 97

Crawford, Earl of, *Crawford Papers*, 1984; 2, 3

English Illustrated Magazine, The (Albert Chevalier, Joseph Hatton, Frederick T. Jane) 35, 42, 83, 96, 99

Fitzgerald, Percy, *London City Suburbs*, 1893; 5, 10, 48, 59, 82

——, *Picturesque London*, 1890; 76

Furniss, Harry, *My Bohemian Days*, 1919; 38, 40, 63, 116, 117

Griffiths, Major Arthur, *Clubs and Clubmen*, 1907; 18

Hare, Augustus J.C., *The Story of My Life*, 1896–1900; 8, 23, 29

Howells, William Dean, *London Films*, 1905; 20, 30, 31, 33, 35, 36, 46, 54, 66, 83, 89, 94, 98

Hueffer, Ford Madox [Ford Madox Ford], *The Soul of London*, 1905; 85

Hutchings, W.W, *London Town Past and Present*, 1909; 19, 24, 31, 36, 38, 45, 63, 93, 111, 119, 121

Illustrated London News, The 15, 16, 18, 19, 22, 33, 35, 37, 39, 45, 48, 49, 50, 52, 58, 61, 63, 68, 70, 73, 77, 90, 96, 98, 102, 110, 111, 117, 120

James, Henry, *English Hours*, 1905; 24, 46, 57, 75

Jones, Henry Festing, *Life of Samuel Butler*, 1919 (Eliza Savage) 21

Loftie, William John, *The Colour of London*, 1914 (Yoshio Markino) 1, 34, 113, 122

——, *London City*, 1891; 53

London, Jack, *The People of the Abyss*, 1903; 11, 46, 101, 104, 109

MacCarthy, Justin, *Charing Cross to St Paul's*, 1893; 52, 53, 54, 55, 56, 115

Macmillan's Magazine (Charles Whibley) 51

Martins, Oliveira, *The England of Today*, 1896; 1, 27, 72, 74

May, Phil, *Gutter-snipes*, 1896; 57

——, *Sketch Book*, 1895; 100

Morand, Paul, *A Frenchman's London*, 1934; 5

Mourey, Gabriel, *Across the Channel*, French ed. 1895, transl. 1896; 38, 42, 44, 86, 110

Nevill, Ralph, and Charles Jerningham, *Piccadilly to Pall Mall*, 1908; 19

Norris, W.E., *A Victim of Good Fortune*, 1894; 90

Pearce, Ernest Harold, *Annals of Christ's Hospital*, 1908; 114

Peters, Carl, *England and the English*, 1904; 21, 54, 69, 88

Punch 93

Punch Almanac, 1898; 67

Raverat, Gwen, *Period Piece*, 1952; 2

Sala, George Augustus, *London Up to Date*, 1894; 2, 8, 25, 40, 91, 122

Sexby, J.J., *The Municipal Parks of London*, 1898; 47

Sheppard, Edgar, *George, Duke of Cambridge*, 1906; 14

Sherwell, Arthur, *Life in West London*, 1897; 5

Sims, George R. (ed.), *Living London*, 1901–3 (Count E. Armfelt, Gilbert Burgess, Henry Leach, Arthur Rutland, P.F. William Ryan, Charles Turner, H.O. Tyman, Desmond Young) 43, 49, 56, 61, 63, 63, 69, 71, 72, 78, 79, 86, 88, 94, 96, 105, 110

——, *My Life*, 1917; 15, 37, 39

Strand Magazine, The (Gilbert Guerdon) 44

Street, George, *A Book of Essays*, 1902; 17

Sturt, George, *Journals*, 1941; 32

Tennent, Dorothy, *London Street Arabs*, 1890; 101

Thornbury, G.W., and Edward Walford, *Old and New London*, 1873–8; 22

Welch, Charles, *Modern History of the City of London*, 1896; 72

Whitten, Wilfred, *A Londoner's Own London*, 1913; 118

Williams, Montagu, *Round London*, 1892; 56, 69, 95, 100, 100

GOLDEN JUBILEE TO GREAT WAR

The most striking discovery about London in 1900 is how similar it was to the London of today. A century ago the City, the West End and the suburbs were fulfilling most of their current functions, and surprisingly often by the same means. The historian writing in the last year of Victoria's pivotal reign could not have said the same about 1800, for during the nineteenth century a revolution had shaken the city. The lighter matter, the people, had been flung to the outskirts, while the dead weight of the offices, the great shops, and the public buildings remained fixed in the centre. But if in 1900 the parts of London had come to rest in a pattern still familiar, very frequently they played their modern roles in eighteenth-century costume. One of the themes of London's history in the twentieth century, a theme already well developed by 1914, was the progressive abandonment of these picturesque properties, with gain to efficiency but loss to amenity.

There have inevitably been many atmospheric changes, literal and metaphorical, during a hundred years. Much the most important ingredient in the popular image of Victorian London is fog. At the time it was widely regarded as a natural feature of the Thames Valley, somewhat exaggerated by the admixture of smoke. Now that coal fires are practically extinct, and only people over forty have any personal memory of a pea-souper, it is obvious that smog must have been nine parts smoke to only one part fog. Its disappearance is the most dramatic change in the atmosphere of London during the past century. Before the Great War it had a constant influence on the life of the city, routinely dimming and shortening both days and seasons.

Contemporary attitudes to the London fog were contradictory. Most people regarded it as a nuisance, and many recognised the threat it posed to health, yet there was a feeling of proprietary pride in the famous phenomenon. There were even groups that regarded it as the glory of London, and were horrified at the idea of smoke abatement. Writers and film-makers could continue to blanket the city with smog long after the nuisance had been eradicated, but for painters it was essential as a living ingredient. It was perhaps appreciated most of all by foreign artists such as Yoshio Markino. 'I am not a chemist', he wrote, 'to analyse the elements of fog. Whether it is healthy or not is not the question for me. The colour and its effect are most wonderful. I think London without mists would be like a bride without a trousseau.'

Such a large city is ill suited to make a striking first impression on visitors. Suburbs are generally tame or ugly, and liable to dull any anticipatory enthusiasm. It was a sad day for London when the Thames ceased to be the usual avenue of approach. That was always calculated to impress. The railway journey from any of the Channel ports had a very different effect. 'The sacred home of the Britons, when observed for the first time, as was the case with me, in the clear light of a glorious June day, inspires fear. The impression is powerful, but I cannot call it agreeable. The sun inhumanely exposes the misery of the poor quarters, with their houses blackened with smoke, hedged about with sticky fogs, with yards, courts, decay, dirt, and an immense sea of little chimneys rising from the slated roofs, like little fingers of pigmies, pointing comically to the sky. The whole is grotesque. It has no grandeur, though one may allow that it possesses immensity.' The immensity conceded by this Portuguese writer in 1892 amazed every stranger.

Visitors and travellers returning from other cities, especially those from Paris, were also greatly struck by the quietness of London. Some even spoke of its silence. This dignified decorum was appreciated in the main, but not in its most exaggerated form, as exhibited during the notorious London Sabbath. That was the terror of all continentals. They saw in it the source of the famous English melancholy, and attributed to it our high rate of suicide. A Sunday in London sorely tempted some French tourists to follow the native example.

INFORMATION
Obliging driver (to country visitor in intense fog): "That there's the Halbert Memorial, but you can't see it!"

Phil May's impression of the London fog, as enjoyed from the top of a garden-seat bus, was sketched in 1893.

*The City social system turned upside down at this warehouse in
French Horn Yard, Crutched Friars, c. 1910. On the first floor are
the top-hatted proprietors, the foremen in their bowlers are on the
second, and the men in flat caps and overalls stand on the third.
Mariner House now occupies this site.*

If the modern Londoner were allowed to step back one
hundred years he would find the stink of the city
insupportable. This was partly caused by the thousands of
horses in the streets and mews. But they were far from the
worst. It was not for nothing that the poor were called the
unwashed. Bathrooms were almost unknown in their houses,
and the idea of local authorities providing public baths was
new and not very widely applied at the start of this period.
The suffering of the wealthy was quite pitiful on occasions
when they were brought into prolonged contact with the
poor, as for example in a police court. 'They are all fragrant
with the same dull, vapid, faintness-engendering, sour, and
almost stifling smell, in which the odours of old rags, old
junk, stale tobacco, stale beer, sawdust, turpentine, and
cheese, seem to be for ever conflicting,' wrote an English
witness in 1894. Foreigners agreed about the unpleasantness
of close contact with the poor, and the most sensitive among

them added that the wealthy might also have bathed more
often.

Although we think of the late Victorian and Edwardian
ages as an oasis of peace and security in a war-torn wilderness
of time, the two emotions that dominated its politics were
guilt and fear. Guilt about poverty at home and fear of a
revolutionary response expressed themselves in social
legislation and an intense interest in charity and missionary
work. Guilt about colonialism and fear of foreign competitors
led alternately to Home Rule and jingoism, pacifism and the
Dreadnought. As the seat of government and the centre of
the empire, London felt these passions and their
consequences in their most intense form. This was especially
the case in the field of social work, which became the
capital's obsession during these decades. Much was done by
private charity, but the increasing interest of government in
social and sanitary questions led it to place ever greater
burdens on the local councils and boards. They expanded
greatly throughout this period.

The perennial subject of a strategic authority for London
was brought to the forefront of politics during the 1890s by a
clash between the venerable Corporation of London and the
hyper-active London County Council. The LCC was
socialistic, puritanical and ambitious. The Corporation of
London was the Corporation of London. The two were
never likely to cooperate harmoniously, and relations reached
freezing point in 1894 when the LCC began a campaign to
extend its jurisdiction to the City. The Corporation retaliated
by suggesting that its own area should be enlarged to include
Southwark. The hopes of the Progressive majority of the
LCC depended on their former chairman, Lord Rosebery,
now Prime Minister. The fall of his government in 1895
saved the ancient constitution of the City. The Conservatives
sought to limit the scope for municipal socialism by a reform
of London's local government, passed in 1899, that
transferred many of the extra powers sought by the LCC to
the individual boroughs.

It was outwardly a religious age, but the spirit was
evaporating. During the last years of Queen Victoria's reign
her capital was essentially a pagan city. In the educated world,
where fashion was everything, God was being discarded along
with beards and frock-coats and other stuffy Victorian props.
When she was nine years old, in 1894, Gwen Raverat was
told in confidence by her younger cousin that 'it was not at
all the thing nowadays to believe in Christianity any more. It
simply wasn't done.' Usually the ruling classes managed to
maintain a formal show of respect for sacred things, for
religion was still seen as a valuable arm of government, but as
the years passed it was not always easy to remain prudent. In
1911, for example, Winston and a very pregnant Clementine
Churchill attended a London fancy dress ball as a cardinal and
a nun. 'Her profile caused disagreeable comments.' It is not
surprising that when they came to grapple with the heathen
world of impoverished London the intellectuals often
regarded their task not as a battle for souls, but as 'a problem
in social ethics, or practical Christianity'.

For many clergymen this practicality took the form of
competing with other churches for the patronage of the

submerged masses. At first the members of the deserving poor were the great prize, but as the struggle to fill the empty pews of slumland intensified Doolittle's distinction seemed less and less important. One East End vicar admitted that 'irreligion is the result of all the bribery: we are all in it; church and chapel are equally bad. It begins with the children – buns to come to Sunday school, and so on; so that they grow up with the idea that the church is simply a milch cow for treats and charity.' By such means an impressive Sunday school roll could always be mustered, but as the children grew up they slipped away one by one.

When ministers resorted to ritual and spectacular services in the hope of attracting a congregation the results were rarely encouraging. Musing on the problem in 1902, Charles Booth was puzzled. 'It does indeed seem strange that the mere attraction of warmth, and light, and music should have so little effect; and one is at times almost driven towards the conclusion that there must be something actually repellent to the people in the pretensions of religion or in the associations of Christian worship.' Increasingly, it seemed, religion 'simply wasn't done', in Bethnal Green any more than in Mayfair.

A more hopeful assault on the roots of poverty was being mounted by the School Board for London, which was making highly visible changes to the appearance of the capital during the 1880s and '90s, and claiming an equal influence on its moral development. Whether education, in England at least, could have any effect whatever, was a question that only

time could answer. The international situation at the end of the century made it a subject of great importance.

Lord Salisbury liked to tell the story of the Chinese statesman who came to propose an ambitious scheme for joint action in the Far East. When Salisbury refused to take the risk the resigned reply was 'I understand; we govern, you and I, two empires on the decline'. The Prime Minister regarded this as an excellent joke, but younger men began to ask themselves, was the Chinaman right? As the last hours of the nineteenth century ticked away Lord Balcarres, who had just celebrated the birth of a son and heir, confided to his diary that 'we face catastrophe: we may be on the eve of changes in our imperial status of which it is impossible to guess the ultimate results . . . Our commercial pre-eminence will be irrevocably lost before our boy goes to school. Yet we have enjoyed a great and in many ways a most glorious century.'

This pessimism was widespread. Its cause was the ever more serious rivalry of the United States and Germany. In the 1860s the position of London at the centre of world commerce, banking and transport had been considered unassailable. Thirty years later it seemed that she would inevitably lose her dominance within a very short period. Of these threats the German was the more alarming to the man in the street because it was at once closer and more alien. The 'dirty German' became a national obsession, and the passions aroused helped set the course for war. At home the

Norman Shaw's rebuilding of the Piccadilly Hotel in such a brutally discordant style between 1905 and 1908 ruined the Quadrant, Nash's masterpiece, and set the course for the destruction of the rest of Regent Street.

*Brompton Road in the late 1880s, when it looked no smarter than the Old Kent Road. The new Harrod's store did not begin to transform the
view until 1901. The hay wagons were probably for Tattersall's, which was on the right, behind Knightsbridge Green.*

scapegoats for commercial decline were the dock companies
and the Thames Conservancy. Our rivals were flourishing, it
was said, because the ports of New York and Bremen and
Antwerp had been modernised while complacent London
had been idle. The response was the establishment of the Port
of London Authority in 1909. In the best traditions of
bureaucracy the first thought of the members was to set about
building a palatial headquarters that took ten years and a
fortune to complete.

The gloomy outlook for trade and the decline in
manufacturing showed no sign of limiting the growth of the
city. The capital tends to have a magnetic influence in any
country, as the field of action for ambition and pleasure. In
the case of London the attraction was multiplied to an

unprecedented extent, because here was the metropolis of
half the world. 'London, that great cesspool into which all
the loungers and idlers of the Empire are irresistibly drained',
increased its population by two-and-a-half million between
1881 and 1911.

Nearly two million of this extra population was added in
the outer suburbs, the parts not officially included in London
until 1963. The poorer immigrants, of course, did not settle
there. The great majority found a first foothold in the slums
of the East End, and under this pressure the more successful
newcomers of previous generations (for nearly all Londoners
are immigrants) moved to the new suburbs. Concern about
the uncontrolled sprawl of London led in this period to the
realisation of Sir Ebenezer Howard's garden city idea,

outlined in 1898 in his book *Tomorrow*. Letchworth, which was developed from 1903, was the first experiment.

The transformation of London into a mere daily workshop created the immense practical problem of providing the millions of commuters with a midday meal. The taverns and chop-houses of the old City could no longer cope, especially when larger numbers of women began to join the daily invasion. The gap was principally filled by the tea-houses established in nearly every street by the Aerated Bread Company (ABC), the British Tea Table Company, the Golden Grain Company, the Express Dairy, and Lyons & Company, with their famous corner houses. There were also numbers of luncheon bars, like Pimm's, where a meal could be taken standing up, and restaurants to suit every pocket.

As the world's largest city London had been a favourite setting for foreign tales of sensational crime and decadence, from Paul Féval's *Les Mystères de Londres* in 1844 to Wedekind's *Pandora's Box* in 1904. The Whitechapel murders of 1888/9 were regarded abroad as a mere confirmation of an ancient ill-repute that 'coloured London for us with gleams of blood and steel'. In fact Jack the Ripper's crimes came at the end of an era, and from that time London entered on a long period of law-abiding respectability. Tourists who visited the East End after 1900 in search of a legendary dissoluteness came away sadly disappointed. They would have been better advised to confine their searches to the West End, where vice continued to flourish. All foreign visitors, even those from supposedly decadent France, were amazed at the extent and blatancy of street prostitution in London, but perhaps even more by its joylessness. The women and their clients seemed equally businesslike, equally sad. As befitted the world's exchange London was a great centre for the import of prostitutes in the late nineteenth century.

The features of London that most often won foreign approval were the police, the horses and the women. Those most constantly damned were the food, the weather and the architecture. The buildings received just as little praise from domestic critics, who were especially severe on Georgian houses, and on anything faced with stucco. After the Law Courts wrangle of the 1880s, which divided the capital into pro-Street and anti-Street factions, Gothic was equally out of favour, and architecture was left with nothing but Queen Anne's skirts to cling to until the rococo and monumental styles offered successive gleams of delusive hope. Between 1897 and 1901 buildings like jubilee cakes gave place to buildings like austere tombstones.

In 1893 Percy Fitzgerald complained of the tameness of the new squares. 'Indeed, this is the general characteristic of most modern architectural attempts in London: reflecting, perhaps, the general indecision and lack of purpose of the time.'

Disraeli had long ago proposed a cure for this plague of dull buildings. 'Shall we find a refuge in a Committee of Taste? Escape from the mediocrity of one to the mediocrity of many? We only multiply our feebleness, and aggravate our deficiencies. But one suggestion might be made. No profession in England has done its duty until it has furnished its victim. The pure administration of justice dates from the deposition of Macclesfield. Even our boasted navy never achieved a great victory until we shot an admiral. Suppose an architect were hanged? Terror has its inspiration as well as competition.'

It is hard to generalise about London, which more than any other city is a collection of ancient settlements linked together in unpredictable ways by the whims of fashion and chance. In 1897 Arthur Sherwell wrote that it 'is like a great, hungry sea, which flows on and on, filling up every creek, and then overspreads its borders, flooding the plains beyond; only, unlike the sea, a city leaves its driftwood behind it' in the form of districts that can no longer be used for the purposes for which they were built. He was thinking particularly of Soho, a luxury suburb of the seventeenth century which had been turned to uses that a puritanical teetotaller could only contemplate with horror. Such fluctuations of function and fashion have continued to be the fate of nearly all London's districts. In 1902 the King's Road, Chelsea, was described as 'shabby and mediocre', Bloomsbury as 'grimy, sordid, squalid', Westminster as 'slummy', and South Kensington as 'ugly'. Bayswater was known as Asia Minor, on account of its popularity with Indian immigrants and visitors.

How did London one hundred years ago compare with our own city? The great Street Improvements had mostly been achieved before 1887, so that only the Kingsway scheme was needed to produce the basic plan of central London as we know it today. The railways were in place, and the Underground network was being rapidly electrified and unified. Motor buses, many of them threading routes still familiar, were ousting the horse-drawn variety, and motor cabs threatening the famous hansoms with extinction. Private cars multiplied with inconceivable rapidity after 1896.

As its other functions dwindled during these decades the City of London was ever more exclusively concerned with finance in all its branches. The West End was ceasing to be predominantly residential and becoming more emphatically than ever before the home of shopping, catering, entertainment and the arts. Specialisation was introducing greater rigidity into the relationship of centre and suburb. Where was it all tending? Towards the modern city, like it or loathe it, the monster that inhales its necessary lungful of workers in the morning and expels it again at five o'clock.

Chapter 1

ROYALTY

There could scarcely be a greater contrast between the state of the monarchy at the end of the nineteenth and twentieth centuries. As Queen Victoria gradually emerged from her long seclusion her popularity rose to unprecedented heights. She was the object of an almost religious veneration that extended into unexpected quarters. Edward Carson, 'the most pitiless prosecutor in the kingdom', was so overcome with emotion when he first saw the Queen in 1897 that he burst into tears. The heir to the throne, perhaps because of his indiscretions rather than in spite of them, was regarded with almost equal popular approval, if with somewhat less respect.

Posterity tends to remember Edward VII as Prince of Wales in the role of Parisian playboy. Yet during the declining years of Queen Victoria the Prince deputised for her constantly. Almost every week Londoners were able to see him opening museums and town halls, attending charitable fairs, or driving from Marlborough House to Buckingham Palace when called upon to act the genial host at a garden party. In late June and July 1890, for example, the Prince opened a hospital and a railway station, visited sick children, and was present when the Princess distributed certificates to nurses at Marlborough House.

Loyalty to the monarchy had ample scope for expression in a period full of great royal events. Two jubilees, the funerals of two monarchs, two coronations, and various weddings and thanksgivings, plus the regular round of political and military ceremonial, gave full opportunity for lavish display. However often the royal processions passed through the streets of the capital the people turned out to cheer with unabated enthusiasm.

It was a shame that so highly valued a jewel should have so base a setting. The Tudors were our only great palace builders. The succeeding dynasties attempted to create an impressive London home for the sovereign, but they always failed. George IV might have done something worthy of the nation if his resources had matched his ambition, but haste and economy had ruined his plans for Buckingham Palace, and the nineteenth and early twentieth-century attempts at improvement only made things worse. In compensation, the approach was improved by the construction of the Admiralty Arch and the conversion of the Mall into a great ceremonial drive, and the Queen Victoria memorial had at least the merit of distracting attention from the new front of the palace.

The last stage in a long and sad story of tinkering was Sir Aston Webb's 1913 refronting in Portland stone, which left Buckingham Palace looking like Selfridge's in The Mall. An apt symbol, perhaps, for the new century: Royalty Reduced! Everything Must Go!

The scene in Broad Sanctuary, outside the west door of the Abbey, during the 1887 Jubilee thanksgiving service. The building on the left, partially concealed by a grandstand, was Westminster Hospital.

A WINDOW IN PALL MALL

Monday, June 13. – Invitation from Lady Wolseley to see the Jubilee Procession from Lord W.'s window at the War Office.

Tuesday, June 21. – At Mary Carlyle's, Chalcot Gardens, Haverstock Hill. – Up at seven, breakfast at quarter to eight. H. and I walk away quietly over Primrose Hill and down Regent's Park, green, almost empty, in the fine summer's morning. As we emerge on the road a troop of the Life Guards passes. Portland Place, Chinese Embassy, two Yellow Dragon flags and the Union Jack between them, lifted a *little higher*. Cavendish Sqr., Hanover Sqr., Piccadilly, – crowd, policemen make way for us across. Then St. James's Sqr. and Pall Mall, cross and to St. James's Park, where we find the back-way into the War Office, shaded with elder and other greenery.

Lord Wolseley's room. – Mr. and Mrs. Frank Holl. Miss Violet Paget introduces herself to me, and we have much talk. She says I was the first person who presented her to the public as authoress: 'I carried about your postcard in my pocket for many days; I was younger then, I'm sorry to say,

than I am now.' She thinks Painters generally talk better than Authors – I don't agree, nor does Mrs. Frank Holl.

Clubs drest up, Junior Carlton opposite, Army and Navy ('*my* club,' says handsome man to his wife), copied from Library at Venice, marble tint 'caused by silica varnish.'

Claret cup and sweet cake. Band, also Ethiopian Serenaders. Sparse red lines of soldiery – police – officials cantering to and fro. Procession at last. Princesses in white, bowing like automatons. Prince of Wales, all gold and feathers; German Crown Prince, tall, in white uniform. The cream horses, and the Queen (white-haired?) Princess of Wales opposite – glittering river of liveries and trappings. Continuous hurrahs – Queen's carriage stops opposite War Office.

Foreign Kings in *covered* carriages – long wait; soldiers march off – all over? – No, here come the Indian Princes – some in livery-stables turn-out; two hansoms – mismanagement somewhere.

Lord Wolseley's room, part of an eighteenth-century dwelling-house, old mantelpiece. Pieces of armour on the walls, weapons, savage spears and shields, Egyptian flag, maps, books.

Downstairs, rough people. H. and I by St. James's Park, past Westminster Abbey, disfigured with stands, and so to

Waterloo station. Home about 5.30 – all well, glad to be back. Bonfires lighted about ten, on Hindhead, Blackdown, and at many points in the Weald. I go up hill with G. and E., and as far as Winkford gate – many fires, rockets, etc. Fire at Aldershot. Hindhead catches fire, and burns all night.

William Allingham, 1887

JUBILEE BALLOONS AND BUNS

June 21, 1887. – I went at 8 a.m. It was not a moment too soon. Cabs charged two pounds to the Abbey, but I walked very comfortably. The tickets had little maps of the Abbey, with the entrance for the bearer marked on each. Mine was by a door on the north-east behind St. Margaret's, and there I waited, with a small crowd, till nine stuck, and some iron gates were opened by the police, when we ran down an awned passage to where a staircase of rough timber led up by the great Norris tomb to our places.

Mine was simply perfect, a splendid place, from whence –

'To see the lords of human kind go by,'

as Goldsmith says. I would not have changed it with any other in the building. In the theatre it would have been the royal box – a little red gallery to hold four, over the tomb of Aylmer de Valence; in front of the gallery on the left of the sanctuary; close above the princesses of Austria, Spain, and Portugal; opposite the kings; with a view of the peers and peeresses in the right transept, and so near the Queen that one could see every play of her expression. My companions were a doctor of music in his red gown and two females of the middle class, who were very good-natured in lending me their glasses.

June 23, 1887. – Yesterday I went at 3 p.m. to Hyde Park. A dense mass of people walled in the vast enclosed space, but all in the utmost good-humour, though many came forward with – 'Oh, do give me your ticket: oh, do now, just for once.' Inside the outer barrier was a second, within which people walked, and whence they saw. I was indignant at first at not being admitted farther, but when I saw the Archbishop of Canterbury refused, was quite contented to share the fate of the first subject in the realm. However, eventually we were both passed into the immense space where the children were playing, not apparently the least over-done by the hot sun, or tired from having been on the move since 10 a.m., and having been provided, on arriving, with nothing but a bag containing a meat-pie, a bun (they say the buns would have reached from London to Brentford in a direct line), and an orange, with instructions to put the bag in their pockets when done with! Each of the 30,000 children also had a 'Jubilee mug' of Doulton ware. Every now and then volleys of tiny coloured balloons were sent up, like flights of bright birds floating away into the soft blue, and, as the royalties arrived, a great yellow balloon, with several people in its car, bore a huge 'Victoria' skywards.

Augustus J.C. Hare, 1887

A FRENCH VIEW OF THE DIAMOND JUBILEE

The filial sentiment the people had for Queen Victoria was the most touching thing to see. Living quietly as she did, they were deprived of the pleasure of seeing her, of the shows in which they delight, and of the various fêtes which would have been profitable commercially. The majority of the people did not complain. They considered that she was free to do as she liked, and there was a certain grandeur in such justice. She was not generous, and she thought of her own family before thinking of the nation; but she was not blamed for this. When any accident happened in any industry she sent the usual message of condolence, and those who received it were satisfied. The Queen represented Mother England, and as such people reverenced her. They were very grateful to her for being a virtuous woman, little realising how difficult it would have been for her to be anything else.

I was at a window on the first floor of the house, when, during a stop in the procession, the Queen's carriage drew up, just opposite us. She was wearing a decent bonnet (which was not an every-day event) and a black silk cape trimmed with white guipure. I gazed with eager curiosity at this woman who could say: 'My subjects, my army, my fleet.' She was making her triumphal journey in that dreamy state which prevents us, at certain moments, from feeling the reality too keenly. It was her apotheosis and yet, in the midst of this strong current of popular love, there was not a single ray of joy or of pride on her face, not a ray of sympathetic feeling, nothing but an expression of nervous timidity. The Queen of England and the Empress of India was, perhaps, a timid woman, and that would explain her way of living. She looked at this crowd, to which she was no longer accustomed, with an astonished and somewhat shrinking expression. The following day, at Kensington, she was either more reassured or she felt more at home, for she smiled in a motherly way at the thousands of children who formed two lines along the road she went. She seemed to me then to be more in communion with her people, and I rejoiced for her and for them. The only country in which it is good to be a Queen or a horse is England, and when I say this, I believe I am paying a tribute to its loyalty and its humaneness.

Augustine Favre de Coulevain, 1906–11

A LEVÉE AT ST. JAMES'S PALACE

The first sensation of the individual to be presented, on entering the palace, is one of blank disappointment. The corridor into which you press with a splendidly apparelled throng before, behind, and around you, presents anything but a palatial aspect. It is, to say the least, somewhat narrow, somewhat dark, and decidedly gloomy. Well; there are many historic palaces in Europe, the approaches to which are the reverse of sumptuous or stately.

The approaches to the splendid saloons of the Pitti Palace at Florence are even meaner and steeper, and not too clean. But you emerge from these shabby stairways to find yourself in

The Queen's carriage passes the William IV statue during the Diamond Jubilee procession, and turns towards London Bridge. The Prince of Wales leads the mounted escort.

apartments of colossal proportions, full of costly furniture, from the ceilings of which hang gigantic chandeliers of Venetian crystals, the cornices and columns of the doorways radiant with gilt mouldings, and the walls hung with priceless tapestry, with historic frescoes, or with gallery pictures by the very greatest masters the world has ever seen. You leave the darksome, intricate, and not too sweetly smelling stairs, and suddenly find yourself in the presence of Michel Angelo and Raffaele, of Titian and Correggio, of Sir Peter Rubens and Sir Anthony Vandyck. That, you will be dejected to find, is not the case at St. James's Palace. Indeed, but for the presence of a couple of the Royal marshalmen in scarlet and gold coatees and black and gold shakos of flower-pot form, and who bear gilt *bâtons* of command in their hands, there is scarcely anything Royal about the vestibule of the palace, which, all things considered, is an edifice not up to any date save that of the most tasteless and the dingiest period of the early Georgian era.

There is, however, a blazing fire, quite regal in its wealth of incandescence; and there you warm yourself for a while, waiting for the barriers to be removed, and for the great crowd of gentlemen in gala attire to ascend the grand staircase into the State apartments. There is a baize-covered counter to your right as you enter, behind which there is a courteous official. You take from a great stack of pasteboards two large blank cards, on which you write your name as legibly as you can; and then you cool your heels, or warm them, as the case may be, for another quarter of an hour.

A barrier is lifted or a glass door opened and you pass into another larger, and somewhat statelier vestibule, where you first become aware of the presence of some of the Royal footmen, duly powdered and in full State livery. By this time you may have grown slightly flustered, and have but an indistinct idea whither you should proceed.

St James's Palace, seen here c. 1905, was not much used as a royal residence after the reign of George III, but was reserved for state and diplomatic functions, and as apartments and offices for courtiers.

Next, you will find yourself at the base of a really handsome staircase, ascending which in serried array you may hear, if you keep your ears open, a good deal of lively small talk as to what is going on, not only in 'smart' London, at the clubs, and in West End *côteries*, but in the 'City'; for here, disguised in the scarlet and carrying the plumed cocked hats of deputy lieutenants or members of the Court of Lieutenancy, are a large contingent of City Aldermen, Common Councillors, Town Clerks, City Solicitors, and so forth.

At the summit of the staircase you find yourself in a large – a very large – apartment, handsome enough from an old-fashioned point of view, and with some rather misty portraits and battle-pieces on the walls. This the guide-books will tell you is the old Presence Chamber. But your remembrance of the guide-books under the excitement of the moment gets very mixed and muddled indeed.

George Augustus Sala, 1894

AN UNLUCKY SPECIMEN

Buckingham Palace is but an unlucky specimen of royal castle-building. There may be some still alive who recall the old Buckingham House pattern. The new palace was one of George IV's many hobbies, and ingulphed enormous sums. From the first it was a failure. The stone is so bad that unless covered by thick coats of paint the whole would become a ruin. When Her Majesty came to the throne it was found to be almost uninhabitable; the kitchen and servants' quarters were close to the Royal apartments. There was no nursery: an essential matter at the moment. It required a sum of £150,000 to put the place in order, and to supply the additions. It is well-nigh forgotten now that the Marble Arch

once stood here, and was the entrance to the palace: a more appropriate site than its present one, as it formed part of an architectural group. The arch has a little history. It was intended to be erected, as it were, *Aux gloires de Georges le Grand*, and an equestrian statue of the monarch was to have been placed on the top. This, somewhat altered, found its way to Trafalgar Square – a good specimen of the wild uncertainties and caprices of officialism. The arch cost £31,000, which was certainly cheap, and the florid iron gates £3,000, which seems dear.

The palace contains a gallery of pictures, comprising no less than seven Rembrandts, seven Rubenses, six Vandykes, nine Cuyps, three Sir Joshuas, besides specimens of many great masters. The public, alas! is not privileged to see these treasures. In the great stables are maintained nearly sixty of the 'state' horses, which include the famous 'creams' – those strange ponderous animals which we see betimes taken out for their exercise: the carriages stored here, including the various state coaches, are about seventy in number.

Few would suppose that the gardens cover forty acres of ground. There is a raised terrace at the back of the palace which commands a full view of the whole; and, by some odd dispensation, 'the Boundary Stone' of St.-Martin's-in-the-Fields is placed here, and on Maunday Thursday the so-called *Beaters of the Bounds* are admitted to strike the stone. Here too is the pavilion which Eastlake, Landseer, Maclise, and a number of other artists, were engaged to paint in fresco, but whose work has since mouldered away from damp and neglect. Will the day ever arrive when these fair gardens will be surrounded with an open gilt-topped railing, like the Tuileries Garden, and the lieges be admitted to walk? There is also a sheet of water, and bosquets *galore*.

Percy Fitzgerald, 1893

A BOLT FROM THE BLUE

23rd June. – The whole of London is decorated for the Coronation, the line of the processions being barricaded with stands for spectators, covered with red cloth. Though the decorations are not generally in the best taste, the general effect is gay, and the grime of London is clothed and put out of sight. Very few modern buildings are not improved by being faced with scaffolding. Immense crowds parade the streets, and traffic is blocked.

24th June. – A bolt has fallen from the blue. The King is ill, has undergone an operation, and the Coronation is postponed. [So little was the misfortune expected that the King and Queen had been photographed, robed and crowned in anticipation. I have one of these photographs by me still. There never was so dramatic a misfortune.]

25th June. – Passing through the Park I found Rotten Row crowded, not a trace of trouble on any face, though the newspapers talk of general gloom. On the contrary, streets are full of gay sightseers, satisfied to look at the decorations since there will be nothing more. Returning after dark I found the Park still crowded, but almost exclusively by lovers who occupied each bench in pairs reposing, according to the naïve London custom, in each other's arms.

Wilfrid Scawen Blunt, 1902

CORONATION TOMFOOLERY

Vivat Rex Eduardus! They crowned a king this day, and there has been great rejoicing and elaborate tomfoolery, and I am perplexed and saddened. I never saw anything to compare with the pageant, except Yankee circuses and Alhambra ballets; nor did I ever see anything so hopeless and so tragic.

To have enjoyed the Coronation procession, I should have come straight from America to the Hotel Cecil, and straight from the Hotel Cecil to a five-guinea seat among the washed. My mistake was in coming from the unwashed of the East End. There were not many who came from that quarter. The East End, as a whole, remained in the East End and got drunk. The Socialists, Democrats, and Republicans went off to the country for a breath of fresh air, quite unaffected by the fact that four hundred millions of people were taking to themselves a crowned and anointed ruler. Six thousand five hundred prelates, priests, statesmen, princes, and warriors beheld the crowning and anointing and the rest of us the pageant as it passed.

I saw it at Trafalgar Square, 'the most splendid site in Europe,' and the very innermost heart of the empire. There were many thousands of us, all checked and held in order by a superb display of armed power. The line of march was double-walled with soldiers. The base of the Nelson Column was triple-fringed with blue-jackets. Eastward, at the entrance to the square, stood the Royal Marine Artillery. In the triangle of Pall Mall and Cockspur Street, the statue of

Jubilee crowds outside Buckingham Palace enjoying Queen's weather in 1897.

The coronation of Edward VII, originally set for 26 June 1902, was finally held on 9 August. The three leading horsemen in this view of the procession passing down Whitehall, were General Sir Alfred Gaselee, Admiral Sir Edward Seymour and Lord Kitchener, figures noticed by Jack London in Trafalgar Square.

George III was buttressed on either side by the Lancers and Hussars. To the west were the red-coats of the Royal Marines, and from the Union Club to the embouchure of Whitehall swept the glittering, massive curve of the 1st Life Guards – gigantic men mounted on gigantic chargers, steel-breastplated, steel-helmeted, steel-caparisoned, a great war-sword of steel ready to the hand of the powers that be. And further, throughout the crowd, were flung long lines of the Metropolitan Constabulary, while in the rear were the reserves – tall, well-fed men, with weapons to wield and muscles to wield them in case of need.

And as it was thus at Trafalgar Square, so was it along the whole line of march – force, overpowering force; myriads of men, splendid men, the pick of the people, whose sole function in life is blindly to obey, and blindly to kill and destroy and stamp out life. And that they should be well fed, well clothed, and well armed, and have ships to hurl them to the ends of the earth, the East End of London, and the 'East End' of all England, toils and rots and dies.

But hark! There is cheering down Whitehall; the crowd sways, the double walls of soldiers come to attention, and into

view swing the King's watermen, in fantastic mediaeval garbs of red, for all the world like the van of a circus parade. Then a royal carriage, filled with ladies and gentlemen of the household, with powdered footmen and coachmen most gorgeously arrayed. More carriages, lords, and chamberlains, viscounts, mistresses of the robes – lackeys all. Then the warriors, a kingly escort, generals, bronzed and worn, from the ends of the earth come up to London Town, volunteer officers, officers of the militia and regular forces; Spens and Plumer, Broadwood and Cooper who relieved Ookiep, Mathias of Dargai, Dixon of Vlakfontein; General Gaselee and Admiral Seymour of China; Kitchener of Khartoum; Lord Roberts of India and all the world – the fighting men of England, masters of destruction, engineers of death! Another race of men from those of the shops and slums, a totally different race of men.

But here they come, in all the pomp and certitude of power, and still they come, these men of steel, these war lords and world harnessers. Pell-mell, peers and commoners, princes and maharajahs, Equerries to the King and Yeomen of the Guard. And here the colonials, lithe and hardy men; and here all the breeds of all the world – soldiers from Canada, Australia, New Zealand; from Bermuda, Borneo, Fiji, and the Gold Coast; from Rhodesia, Cape Colony, Natal, Sierra Leone and Gambia, Nigeria, and Uganda; from Ceylon, Cyprus, Hong-Kong, Jamaica, and Wei-Hai-Wei; from Lagos, Malta, St. Lucia, Singapore, Trinidad. And here the conquered men of Ind, swarthy horsemen and sword wielders, fiercely barbaric, blazing in crimson and scarlet, Sikhs, Rajputs, Burmese, province by province, and caste by caste.

And now the Horse Guards, a glimpse of beautiful cream ponies, and a golden panoply, a hurricane of cheers, the crashing of bands – 'The King! the King! God save the King!' Everybody has gone mad. The contagion is sweeping me off my feet – I, too, want to shout, 'The King! God save the King!' Ragged men about me, tears in their eyes, are tossing up their hats and crying ecstatically, 'Bless 'em! Bless 'em! Bless 'em!' See, there he is, in that wondrous golden coach, the great crown flashing on his head, the woman in white beside him likewise crowned.

Jack London, 1903

A GOOD BLOKE

It is a fine thing to consider, and one as to which the English may well pride themselves, that King Edward's life is so secure as it is. The writer freely confesses that it has more than once surprised him to find that, from the kerbstone even, it would have been no difficult matter to make an attempt upon it – and that with many reasonable chances of successfully accomplishing such a gratuitous crime. So fearlessly unprotected does he go about amongst his people, that it would almost appear as though he actually courted destruction at the hands of a fanatic or a madman. But it is not so. His personal guardians are the people who stand along the kerbstones; his security does not lie in the brace of troopers who precede his carriage on ordinary occasions. It lies in the affection of his people.

The writer remembers seeing his carriage for the first time, from the top of an omnibus, as it drove away from Charing Cross one windy evening. The two mounted policemen were the most noticeable feature of the equipage, and their smart appearance prompted interrogation of the bus-driver as to who might be inside the closed carriage.

Edward VII's carriage turning from the Victoria Station forecourt into Buckingham Palace Road in 1901.

'What-ho!' was the reply. 'Don't cher know? That's 'is most gryshus!'

'What! the King?'

'Yuss; that's 'im, right enough.'

One expressed surprise at the fact that his escort was so small, so apparently inadequate. It was no more than the escort of a State Governor at home. How were they to look after the King, in case of a row? The driver laughed.

'W'y, 'oo's goin' to 'urt 'im, mister? There ain't no one in London 'ud touch a 'air of 'is 'ead. 'E's a good bloke, 'e is.'

Now that was one way of putting it. It may not be usual, in old king-equipped countries, to refer to the head of the State as a 'bloke'. Even to an irreverent Australian it sounds a little incongruous. But it is, one believes, perfectly true. And its truth is a matter for congratulation no less to King Edward than to the nation.

J.H.M. Abbott, 1905

ALL DUKES TO-DAY

An amusing incident occurred at the Press Bazaar for the London Hospital in 1898. 'I had forgotten,' writes Mr. Sydney Holland, 'to tell His Royal Highness which door to arrive at. There was a tremendous crush and a huge crowd waiting to get in. It was an anxious time, as the Queen was just due and the crowd looked dangerous because of its numbers. So I sent out word that no one else was to be admitted in any circumstance. The Queen arrived at her special entrance – reserved for him too – and I was conducting her round when I heard a noise as of an earthquake. Up came the Duke; he almost seized me by the collar and forgetful of the Queen being present said, "What does this mean? I – I – I as President of the Hospital was refused entrance." I tried to explain. "You're a d—d bad organiser – no excuse can be received – you ought to be shot!" and so on, only worse. It was useless for me to try and

The London Hospital, Whitechapel Road, in 1891. It was moved here in 1759, when this was practically open country, but had been extended and altered many times since then, most recently in 1890.

explain. In fact I did not know then what had happened. The Queen was much amused and said, "You seem to have annoyed the Duke!" When I heard what had happened I am bound to admit that enough had occurred to ruffle the equanimity of a man not blessed with what one might call a very even temper. The dear old Duke, keen to help the Hospital, had arrived in plenty of time and had found the huge crowd blocking the doors. He had forced his way through and had at last reached the door. A young policeman guarded the door. He hammered at it. The young man opened it, "What do you want?" "I want to come in." "Well, you can't, Mr. Holland has sent orders that no one else is to be admitted." "D—n Mr. Holland, I am the Duke of Cambridge!" "Oh! I daresay," said the policeman, "we are all Dukes to-day!" Just imagine His Royal Highness's feelings! It took him three weeks to forgive me.'

Edgar Sheppard, 1906

The long and stormy career of Queen Victoria's impetuous cousin the Duke of Cambridge as Commander-in-Chief of the Army was ended by his enforced retirement in 1895. He is seen here speaking at the banquet at the Café Monico given on the occasion by the War Office staff. Lord Wolseley, the new Commander-in-Chief, is on the right.

THE DUKE OF CAMBRIDGE AGAIN

At the beginning of June 1889 I returned from a brief holiday in Switzerland to find that in my absence I had been assaulted by the Duke of Cambridge, and that the assault of the Duke upon 'Mr. George Sims, journalist, and a member of the staff of a Sunday paper,' had been the subject of a question in the House of Commons.

The assault, it seemed, had taken place when the Duke was at a review of the Fire Brigade at Whitehall, at which the Prince and Princess of Wales were present.

There had been a rush of the crowd, and in that rush Mr. George Sims, the journalist, had been pushed against the Duke of Cambridge, and the fiery Duke had seized the journalist by the throat and shaken him 'like a rat.'

As I happened at the time of the assault to have been on the summit of Pilatus I could not understand how the Duke, even if his arm had been longer than that of coincidence, had reached so far as from Whitehall to the summit of the mountain where is the tarn in which Pontius Pilate is supposed to have drowned himself.

When I found certain provincial newspapers giving a short account of my life and work in connexion with the Commander-in-Chief's attack upon me, I was compelled to write a disclaimer to the daily papers.

It was some time before I was able to convince the sympathetic American Press that the assault had not been committed upon me, but upon Mr. George E. Simms, a young journalist on the staff of the *Sunday Sun*.

In the meantime the affair had assumed sensational proportions. Mr. Simms had applied for a summons at a police-court, and the magistrate had refused to listen to his application.

Then Mr. Abinger, on behalf of Mr. Simms, went before the Lord Chief Justice and Mr. Justice Hawkins for an order calling upon Mr. Bridge, a Metropolitan police magistrate, to show cause why he should not hear and determine Mr. Simm's application, and after a long and legal argument the Lord Chief Justice decided that Mr. Bridge had not exercised the discretion which he was bound to exercise judicially, and therefore the rule must be granted, and Mr. Justice Hawkins concurred.

Then the American Press, still believing that I was the Sims, favoured me with columns of sympathy. One leading journal headlined its article, 'Royalty Under Arrest; Queen Victoria's cousin, the Commander-in-Chief of the British Empire, must answer in a police-court for an assault upon George R. Sims, the well-known journalist and dramatic author.'

And all this beautiful sympathy was unfortunately wasted. I was not the Sims.

A year or two afterwards I was introduced to the Duke at one of the Earl's Court exhibitions, and he evidently remembered the affair, for he smilingly said, 'I think you are the George Sims I did *not* assault?'

George R. Sims, 1917

Chapter 2

SOCIETY

Society is always in decline. In every generation the elders of the West End have complained that the men are less witty than in their halcyon days, the women less beautiful, the manners less polished, the charmed circle less exclusive. Between 1887 and 1914 the proponents of this view could marshal an unusually impressive array of evidence. The aristocrats who had led Society for so long, now that land gave them a position and prevented them from keeping it up, were undoubtedly being outstripped in the race for wealth by the great manufacturers and financiers. Their London homes were becoming too expensive to maintain, and the era of demolitions was at hand. In Piccadilly and Park Lane the typical resident was no longer a duke but a Jewish banker.

One curious result of the comparative impoverishment of the landowning classes was a vast increase in the number of luxury flats in London. Those who had traditionally maintained both a country seat and a town house were looking to economise by moving to something more modest. For a duke this might mean swapping a palace by the park for a mansion in one of the fashionable squares, but for the obscure squire who had struggled to afford a tiny house in a Mayfair side street a flat was now the only alternative to giving up London altogether. In a contracting market for large houses the block of flats also became a more attractive investment for the landlords. This had a great effect upon the London season, for in every circle the quantity and quality of entertainment was being reduced. Fewer people had the ability to give lavish receptions and balls, and for the flat dwellers even dinner parties had to be contracted to a much more modest scale.

By 1914 the London clubs had passed their heyday. The minor ones that had been established during the fat years of the mid-nineteenth century were now losing members and either closing or amalgamating, and even the great clubs found their waiting lists growing shorter. This was caused partly by the financial troubles of the landed gentry, and partly by changes of fashion and taste. The classic clubman had lived modestly in Mayfair or St James's and made White's or the Athenaeum his real home. With more and more potential recruits living in the suburbs the need for a London club had diminished. The rise of golf and motoring as popular pastimes also took their toll. In this the clubs were a microcosm of Society, which was becoming diluted as its membership was dispersed.

Marlborough House, the modest London home of the great Duke, was extensively altered and enlarged in the early 1860s for the Prince of Wales. During his forty-year wait for the succession the Prince made it the centre of that Society on which Buckingham Palace had shut its doors.

IMPECUNIOUS ST. JAMES'S

Mayfair and St. James's have different atmospheres, the one from the other, now. Mayfair suggests plutocracy. St. James's is rather impecunious than otherwise: there are so many stray men of poor fortunes in its attics. St. James's Square and a few houses in St. James's Place are about the only harbourage of whole families, plutocratic or otherwise: the rest is clubs and shops and lodging-houses. In the ten years or so that my acquaintance with St. James's Street has been constant, it seems to be growing less dignified. There is – it seems to me – more blatant noise of newspaper-boys, more orange-peel, more bits of paper in the street than was once the case. But St. James's remains the district of all others in town where a stray man should live, unless he live in the Temple. It has associations and a pleasant atmosphere of a kind even now. The Palace and the guards outside it, and the house across the way, give it dignity for the circuit of a rood or so. It does not swarm with miscellaneous crowds on Sunday, as does Piccadilly, but there is always some interest of humanity as you stroll about or look out of a club window. The milk is carried round by women with the pails slung across their shoulders; they suggest a game of Arcadia. There is a gratification also in living near St. James's Square, certainly the most dignified square in the town. I have never been able to understand how anybody not the twentieth duke of his family and the possessor of several estates in the country can presume to live in St. James's Square, and I have always felt it to be an honour and a pledge of a dignified life to live, as it were, round the corner of it. It speaks of ducal lines. And so

This view up St James's Street in 1900 was apparently photographed from the window of the Conservative Club. The tall white building at the corner of King Street, then the Junior Army and Navy Club, is now an office block, with the inevitable greedy attic storey added.

the Palace speaks of Courts, though to be sure the last Court interesting to me was held in Whitehall. But I am drifting back to old times: enough to say that St. James's is the proper district for your single man.

George Street, 1902

CLUB ECCENTRICS AND LUNATICS

The ways of particular members, their habits, tastes, foibles, will be thrown up into strong relief, where existence is congregate and life public. We may know little of a man's private affairs, what his income is exactly, or even approximately, or how he earns it; what he does, indeed, 'by daylight,' as the saying goes; whether he is married, or has been, or separated, or lives *maritalement*; whether he owns a palatial mansion, or is satisfied with a modest bedroom in some shady corner of Clubland. But the manner in which he personally comports himself, his demeanour and conduct, his dress and appearance, the opinion he holds and proclaims, are matters of general knowledge, the better and more widely appreciated the more strongly pronounced and peculiar. Many exhibit no more than the milder forms of eccentricity, quaint traits a little out of the common, but sufficiently marked to win them good-humoured but depreciatory criticism. 'Rum chap,' we murmur pityingly, recognising that the same may be said of ourselves, and that numbers are in the same boat. A few, however, are more distinctly 'dotty'; palpably maniacs, men whose mental deficiencies amount to

aberration of intellect and positive lunacy. Every club owns one or two members who might at any time be certified as insane if it was worth the trouble, or indeed, requisite, so as to secure the general comfort, and afford protection to the whole body. As a rule they are harmless; only now and again do they occasion serious inconvenience, or become really dangerous.

A very marked and notable case is recorded in the tradition of one well-known club. A member, who had been long out of sight, re-appeared in what had once been his favourite haunt, and without eliciting special comment; for men may come and men may go, but the club flows on for ever, unruffled and unconcerned. He was hailed with the usual careless greeting: 'Halloa! Not seen you lately,' or some more callous, heartless wretch may add: 'We thought you were dead.' Here the unfortunate absentee had only been laid by in a living tomb. He had been under restraint, from which he had succeeded in escaping, and had now come up to London and walked straight into his club. While waiting for the lunch he forthwith ordered, he called loudly for a bowl of ice, and proceeded to pile the pieces upon the convex top of his bald crown, from which they rolled down continually on to his own and the neighbouring tables. Meanwhile, he glared fiercely at the servants and condemned them in wild, truculent terms; when at last he demanded a carving-knife to eat his oysters with, he had to find it for himself, as no one dared approach him. A special messenger was promptly despatched to Scotland Yard; but the police inspector who came in answer to the summons declared that he was unable to act, for the troublesome member was actually in his own

The hall of the Carlton Club in Pall Mall, as rebuilt in 1854 to the designs of Sydney Smirke and George Basevi, is seen here in 1890. The club moved to its present St James's Street premises when its Pall Mall home was destroyed by bombing during the Second World War.

house, the club being to all intents and purposes his private residence. A hasty conference was held, a couple of magistrates and two doctors were sought out and invited to sign an order for removal to an asylum, but hesitated to take the responsibility, and the lunatic remained master of the situation. He had the coffee-room to himself and ranged to and fro furiously, brandishing the carving-knife, while the terrified servants stared at him from the doors. In the end he walked out unmolested into the street, where he fell into the clutches of a keeper who had come in search of him.

Major Arthur Griffiths, 1907

THE LAST OF THE PICCADILLY LOUNGERS

For the last twenty-five years Piccadilly, once frequented by many characters known for their eccentricity of gait and attire, has become quite a humdrum thoroughfare, the last lounger of marked individuality and leisured independence having been the Piccadilly goat, an animal which about ten or twelve years ago was wont to wander, pensive and unattended, along this old street, in which it was so perfectly at home, stopping occasionally to browse on such railings as, in spite of many former ineffectual attacks, seemed likely to afford some promise of refreshment.

From time to time, when wearied with its ill-success in

this direction, it would wander into clubs. In the hall of one it ate up the tape; at another it walked upstairs into the coffee-room, where it created a stampede.

As a rule, however, seemingly conscious of its responsibilities as the last of the Piccadilly loungers, it was perfectly content to stroll from the Mews in which it had its home to some point of vantage where on sunny days it could bask in dignified contemplation.

Ralph Nevill and Charles Jerningham, 1908

CROOKED, IRREGULAR, AND INCONGRUOUS

Park Lane, in the reign of Queen Anne a desolate bye-road known as Tyburn Lane, has become proverbial as the centre of fashionable London, the desired haven alike of a proud aristocracy and of our *nouveaux riches*. Yet it has neither symmetry nor the faintest semblance of architectural unity. At its southern end it dwindles down almost to the width of an alley, at scarce any point has it noble breadth, it is neither straight nor curved, but simply crooked. And though it contains some beautiful and dignified houses, most of the older buildings, judged as architecture, have no merit in themselves, nor are they congruous with each other. Many of them have not so much as a foot of ground between them and the roadway, and here and there one comes upon a cluster of

The shady side of Piccadilly in 1895, when the policeman apparently had so little official business to attend to in this favoured spot that he was happy to walk a dowager's dog.

them huddled together as closely as the houses in some mean street. Finally it is numbered with an inconsecutiveness which, though baffling, sorts excellently with its other characteristics, nor is it surprising to find that one group of houses turn their backs upon it, and prefer to be known as Seamore Place. The fact is that Park Lane is so much desired partly because it is so irregular and so incongruous – because it is neither street nor avenue, square nor crescent – because it is what it styles itself, a lane. Its other and more obvious distinction is that, except at its Piccadilly end, it lies quite open to Hyde Park, being built upon only the eastern side.

W. W. Hutchings, 1909

THE MANY OR THE FEW?

The greater parks are open to the public, but the squares are enclosed by tall iron fences, and locked against the general with keys of which the particular have the keeping in the houses about them. It gave one a fine shiver of exclusion as populace, or mob, to look through their barriers at children playing on the lawns within, while their nurses sat reading, or pushed perambulators over the trim walks. Sometimes it was even young ladies who sat reading, or, at the worst, governesses. But commonly the squares were empty, though the grass so invited the foot, and the benches in the border of

the shade, or round the great beds of bloom, extended their arms and spread their welcoming laps for any of the particular who would lounge in them.

I remember only one of these neighborhood gardens which was open to the public, and that was in the poor neighborhood which we lodged on the edge of, equally with the edge of Belgravia. It was opened, by the great nobleman who owned nearly the whole of that part of London, on all but certain days of the week, with restrictions lettered on a board nearly as big as the garden itself; but I never saw it much frequented, perhaps because I usually happened upon it when it was locked against its beneficiaries. Upon the whole, these London squares, though they flattered the eye, did not console the spirit so much as the far uglier places in New York, or the pretty places in Paris, which are free to all. It can be said for the English way that when such places are free to all they are not so free to some, and that is true. In this world you have to exclude either the many or the few, and in England it is rather the many who are excluded. Being one of those shut out, I did not like the English way so well as ours, but if I had had keys to those locks, I should not now dare ask myself which principle I should have preferred. It would have been something like choosing between popular government and family government after having been created one of the governing families.

William Dean Howells, 1905

The modern Londoner, used to Park Lane as little better than a motorway, may find difficulty in imagining it as a real lane, narrow and crooked. This photograph, taken c. 1912 from Marble Arch, should help. But things were already changing. The entrance to the park had lately been set back, and in Oxford Street, just out of shot to the left, a cinema had been built.

The eastern side of Berkeley Square in the late 1880s, before the age of demolition began. The photographer was looking up the hill from the shade of the Lansdowne House garden. Not one of these houses survives.

THE AMENITIES OF PORTLAND PLACE

Apropos of odious creatures, I saw Mr. Gladstone last week. He came out of Lord Selborne's house in Portland Place. He was looking dreadfully cross and very yellow. He seemed undecided as to where he should cross the street, and he stared at me in a helpless sort of way as if he expected me to offer him some advice on the matter; but, as there was no possibility of putting him in the way of being run over, I refrained from giving an opinion. The crossings about Portland Place are so stupidly safe.

Eliza Savage, 1880

THE DOGGED PURSUIT OF PLEASURE

The current runs in one distinct direction, towards a long sideboard in a room to the back covered with refreshments of all kinds, more especially champagne, various cups, seltzers and lemonades. Before this table there is a continuous, silent, but none the less stubborn fight going on, similar to that for the boats on a sinking ocean steamer. The first business of the agenda is to get near the refreshments; next to get hold of a glass of champagne, and the last, but by no means the least, to swallow it before a neighbour capsizes it with his elbow over our snow-white shirt front.

There is many a slip –

The immense width of Portland Place, which William Pett Ridge thought would make a fine football pitch, is seen here at the junction with Duchess Street, c. 1910.

The luxurious reception rooms of Brooke House, Park Lane, the home of the Liberal politician Lord Tweedmouth, photographed in 1902. On his death in 1909 the mansion was bought by King Edward's friend Sir Ernest Cassel. It was demolished in 1933.

This happily accomplished, we try to solve a second and no less difficult technical problem, viz., to escape from this crowd to work our way back to our coat and to regain the street. It is advisable for this purpose, like the sailing vessel in the tropics watches for a current of air, so to look for and fall in with a countercurrent to take us out of this struggling mass.

With a bit of good luck we at last reach the outside without broken bones.

This is a typical London reception. The social purpose is a mystery to me, unless its function be to prepare us poor mortals already here in this world for purgatory in the hereafter, or to teach us what hell must be like.

But on we go, our course it not yet run, the evening is not yet over. It is now a quarter to twelve, the very time for the ball in Park Lane, the next number on our programme. The introduction is the same as at the dinner-party and reception, only in this case our names are not called out into the hall, from where the sound of waltzing reaches us. The unlucky victims of the evening, the hosts, are standing at the door, apparently worn out, but bidding us welcome with the inevitable smile. We see dancing pairs closely surrounded by a rigidly stagnant, watching crowd, resembling nothing more than the spluttering in a fast freezing stream. Here, too, for a space accommodating about 150 persons a thousand invitations have been issued and, as a consequence, we are almost suffocated. As soon as the dance is finished the couples hurry into the refreshment room, in which

the same conditions prevail as we noted in the case of the reception; some guests sit on the stairs, window-sills or any odd corners where they carry on a sweet flirtation, forgetful of the stifling atmosphere, and rendering our hard fight for the open still harder. At last we breathe the fresh night air and hurry to our club to refresh ourselves with a glass of iced whisky and soda and to recover from the fatigues and perils of the evening, before seeking our well-earned repose.

Carl Peters, 1904

TIME-DEFYING DORCHESTER HOUSE

Dorchester House, the residence of Mr. R. S. Holford, the gardens of which face Park Lane on the one side, and Dean Street on the other, is one of the handsomest of the many modern mansions of London. It is in the ornate Italian style, and stands on the site of an older mansion of the same name, which was one of the residences of the late Marquis of Hertford, who died there in 1842.

The present mansion was built in 1851–2, from the architectural designs of Mr. Lewis Vulliamy. It is faced with Portland stone, and in plan forms a parallelogram, about 105 feet wide by 135 feet in depth, very nearly the size of Bridgewater House. The grand staircase is of marble, and the interior generally is fitted up with great completeness. 'This mansion,' says the *Builder*, 'is a very good specimen of masonry, and is built for long endurance. The external walls are 3 feet 10 inches thick, with a cavity of about 5 inches, and the proportion of stone is great, and the bonders numerous; the stones are all dowelled together with slate

After the death of its millionaire creator Dorchester House was mothballed until the government rented it in 1895 (the date of this drawing) as a residence for the Shahzada, son of the Ameer of Afghanistan, during his state visit to England.

dowells; and throughout, the greatest care appears to have been taken by the architect to ensure more than usually sound construction. If the New Zealander, who is to gaze on the deserted site of fallen London in some distant time to come, sees nothing else standing in this neighbourhood, he will certainly find the weather-tinted walls of Dorchester House erect and faithful, and will, perhaps, strive to discover the meaning of the monogram which appears on the shield beneath the balconies, 'R.S.H.', that he may communicate his speculations to some 'Tasmanian Society of Antiquaries', perhaps not more pugnacious, if less erudite, than our own.'

Edward Walford, 1876

July 7. – Miss Holford was married this afternoon to Mr. Benson at St. George's before an immense crowd. There was a great breakfast afterwards – though so late – at Dorchester House, where all London flocked through the rooms to admire the presents, which were indescribably splendid. The scene on the beautiful white marble staircase was charming, especially when the bride went away, her father and mother leading her down on either side, and all the tiny bridesmaids and pages – nieces and nephews between six and seven – gambolling in front, with huge baskets of dark red roses. Above, under the circular arches, between the pillars of coloured marbles, and against a golden wall background, the overhanging galleries were filled with all the most beautiful women in London leaning over the balustrades.

Augustus J. C. Hare, 1887

ASQUITH RATHER OUT OF IT

1st May. – To Grosvenor Square, where I found Sir Charles Tennant very important over his daughter's approaching marriage. 'It has gone on now,' he said, 'for a year and a half, at first all on Asquith's side, but now Margot is sincerely attached to him. She has smartened him up wonderfully, you would hardly know him.' Upon which in walks Asquith, a little smooth-shaved middle-aged man, with a beatific smile on his face, as of one to whom Heaven's doors have been opened. He reminded me very cordially of our former meetings on Home Rule platforms, and in answer to my congratulations, said, 'Indeed you have reason to congratulate me.' Sir Charles gives his daughter £2,000 a year and a house in Cavendish Square. They are to spend the honeymoon in Caroline Grosvenor's house, 30, Upper Grosvenor Street, which they have rented for the season.

10th May. – Margot's wedding day, showery and cold, but with occasional gleams of sunshine. St. George's crammed to the ceiling with the gayest world of the gay. It is the only church in London I have the smallest romance about, but to me it is interesting and touching from the vast number of marriages it has seen (including my own). It is old-fashioned, with nice comfortable pews, and none of the tawdry Gothic rubbish they are fond of elsewhere. De Staal was there in the same pew with us, and there were Rosebery and I believe all the Ministers, and Gladstone, who came in late and was cheered outside, and Arthur Balfour. Margot was pale, very pale, but firm and decided, Asquith much smartened up. A great crush in the Tennant house afterwards in Grosvenor Square, Margot surrounded by a crowd of women friends. She drove away in a slatey-blue dress, an apple-green straw hat and dark-blue flowers.

The Illustrated London News *depiction of the Asquith wedding shows the not always terribly happy couple (in futurity at least) encircled by all the leading statesmen of the day.*

17th July. – A brilliant luncheon with Margot and her husband at 30, Upper Grosvenor Street, and I took her her Wedding Ode, which I had written for her amusement. The other guests were Mrs. Grenfell, Mrs. Daisy White, Ribblesdale, his brother Reggie Lister, and Oscar Wilde, all immensely talkative, so that it was almost like a breakfast in France. Asquith alone rather out of it. I sat next to him and was rather sorry for him, though he was probably happy enough. Afterwards, when the rest had gone away, Oscar remained, telling stories to me and Margot.

Wilfrid Scawen Blunt, 1894

FOUR PRIME MINISTERS

In George Street, on the south side of the square, built about the same time as the square and still little altered, is the church of St. George, long famous for its fashionable marriages, though of late years it has been to some extent supplanted in this respect by St. Paul's, Knightsbridge.

The marriage of Mr. Asquith, then Home Secretary, to Miss Margot Tennant (May 10th, 1894) was remarkable from the fact that the register was signed by the Prime Minister, Lord Rosebery, by the ex-Prime Minister, Mr. Gladstone, who had retired from office a few weeks before, and by a future Prime Minister, Mr Arthur Balfour.

W. W. Hutchings, 1909

THE ROTTEN ROW CIRCUS

In Hyde Park I should follow the water-side, or the Row, or any other fancy of the occasion; liking best perhaps, after all, the Row in its morning mood, with the mist hanging over the dark red course, and the scattered early riders taking an identity as the soundless gallop brings them nearer. I am free to admit that in the Season, at the conventional hours, the Row becomes a weariness (save perhaps just for a glimpse once a year, to remind one's self how much it is like Du Maurier); the preoccupied citizen eschews it and leaves it for the most part to the gaping barbarian. I speak of it now from the point of view of the pedestrian; but for the rider as well it is at its best when he passes either too early or too late. Then, if he be not bent on comparing it to its disadvantage with the bluer and boskier alleys of the Bois de Boulogne, it will not be spoiled by the fact that, with its surface that looks like tan, its barriers like those of the ring on which the clown stands to hold up the hoop to the young lady, its empty benches and chairs, its occasional orange-peel, its mounted policemen patrolling at intervals like expectant supernumeraries, it offers points of real contact with a circus whose lamps are out. The sky that bends over it is frequently not a bad imitation of the dingy tent of such an establishment. The ghosts of past cavalcades seem to haunt the foggy arena, and somehow they are better company than the mashers and elongated beauties of current seasons. It is not without interest to remember that most of the salient figures of English society during the present century – and English society means, or rather has hitherto meant, in a large degree English history – have bobbed in the saddle between

The junction of the carriage road and Rotten Row at Hyde Park Corner, c. 1900. As an exclusive Society institution the Park was undermined by the decline of deference at the turn of the century, and killed, like so much else, by the triumph of the motor car.

Apsley House and Queen's Gate. You may call the roll if you care to, and the air will be thick with dumb voices and dead names, like that of some Roman amphitheatre.

Henry James, 1888

AN EXPENSIVE FLAT

All over western, south-western, and north-western London, huge mansions are rising up in the shape of residential flats. I have occupied one in Screech Owl Street, S.W. [Victoria Street], during the last five years. Here it is! Large, well-erected house – I have never cared to inquire how many storeys high – without the slightest suspicion of jerry-building about it. When I first went to live there the mansion was destitute of a lift; but that convenience has since been added to it, and the landlord carefully popped on ten pounds additional to the rent, as a solatium for the concession of the elevator.

The kitchen and pantry are at the right hand of the entrance hall, and for four servants there is only one bedroom, so I am obliged to colonise one of them out, by taking a lodging for him in the neighbourhood.

Altogether, including kitchen and bath-room, we have nine moderately-sized rooms at our disposal. The front rooms look on to Screech Owl Street, and are light enough; the back rooms are somewhat dark, not through any fault of our landlord, but because there rises in the rear of us another gigantic block of residential flats, brand-new ones.

It cost me a pretty penny to get into this highly eligible flat. I was a widower when I went there, and therefore needed no boudoir drawing-room, but I wanted a long gallery for the bookcases holding what I call my 'swell-books'; that is to say, the rare ones, the editions *de luxe* and the triumphs of bookbinding which I possess; to say nothing of some pictures and bronzes and porcelain and other bric-à-brac. So, with the permission of the landlord, I had an arch cut between one room and another, and draped it with tapestry curtains, which could be closed if required. Altogether, what with taking away an old, elaborate, and dreadfully rusty bath apparatus and substituting a bath up to date for it; what with money paid to the builder, and the upholsterers, and the roller-blind makers; what with cutting up large carpets to lay down in small rooms, looking to the gas installation, selling old articles of furniture at a loss and buying new ones; what with buying innumerable yards of brass rods for hanging pictures and prints on, and especially what with paying the workmen's time during the weeks upon weeks they were occupied in my nine rooms; and, finally, what with the payment of eighty pounds to the obliging firm who moved my books and curios without so much as losing a volume or breaking a teacup, I found that it cost me close upon a thousand pounds to become the occupant of the flat in question, at a rental of two hundred and ten pounds a year, plus ten pounds additional for the use of the lift, and plus, at the present, another twelve pounds per annum for the rent of the lodgings of the servant who sleeps out.

Now I came to Screech Owl Street from Mecklenburg Square, W.C., a large roomy house of twelve rooms. I could have entertained five-and-twenty guests in the dining-room, and given

a ball to a hundred and fifty in the two drawing-rooms. In a back bedroom on the second floor I could find room for three thousand books, and altogether, when I left, I could comfortably house ten thousand volumes. Since that period, of course, I have bought many more books, but there is absolutely no room in the nine handsome cupboards in Screech Owl Street for anything else of any nature whatsoever – furniture, books, curios, or bronzes.

Finally, in justice, let this picture of a strictly up-to-date flat be completed with one more observation. It cannot be denied that flats are cosy in winter time; and perhaps no more comfortable dwelling than a handsome flat could be devised for the home of a young married couple devoted to society, who are constantly out and about at balls, dinners, and receptions, and entertain very little at home. And again for a bachelor, his valet and housekeeper, a flat is a very comfortable domicile; but for large families, or busy people, whose business in life has to be carried on entirely at home, I contend that a house is a far more advantageous dwelling, as well as infinitely more comfortable than a flat.

George Augustus Sala, 1894

Imperial Mansions was a block of comparatively luxurious flats designed by the firm of Martin and Purchase, and built in 1889. It was demolished in 1961 as part of what was impishly called the St Giles's Circus Improvement. If it seems to you not very beautiful, consider that Centre Point now occupies the site, and think again.

Chapter 3

TOURISM

As the world metropolis of the nineteenth century, London had been visited throughout by large numbers of tourists, but it was only in the last decades that any trouble was taken to attract them. Until then the foreigner was apt to find accommodation scarce and unsatisfactory, and the population suspicious. Those that settled in London usually ended, like Henry James, in loving it in spite of its faults, but the fleeting stranger was more often sent away hostile and only reluctantly impressed.

When facilities for tourists did begin to improve in the last years of the century the impetus for change came as much from foreign as from British enterprise. American hoteliers and shopkeepers and French and Italian restaurateurs played a prominent part in the movement that transformed London's skyline and temper between 1890 and 1910.

The round of tourist sights was very much the same a hundred years ago as it is today, except where London's memorials and things of fame have suffered from twentieth-century violence. All foreign and provincial visitors did the familiar tour of Westminster Abbey and St Paul's, the Houses of Parliament and Buckingham Palace, the Tower of London and the Monument, the Horse Guards and Speakers' Corner. The museums and galleries, the parks and the zoo, were all much the same then as now. Even the hideous idea of a Jack the Ripper tour, which might seem peculiarly modern, is really nothing new. A Portuguese tourist was taken on something very similar, by a detective, in 1892. A little East End slumming was then an essential part of any serious itinerary. Some new attractions added to the repertoire during this period were Tower Bridge in 1894, Westminster Cathedral, begun in 1895 and still unfinished today, and the Tate Gallery, opened in 1897.

Madame Tussaud's exhibition hall in Marylebone Road a few years after it was opened in 1884. The building was severely damaged by fire in 1925, and by bombing in 1940, and now only part of the façade survives, heavily altered.

BABYLON

From the verandahs of the Savoy, London presents a different aspect. The Thames there makes a wide bend, convex opposite the left bank, upon which I was. Looking downwards I saw at a little distance Waterloo Bridge, of stone, covered with people and vehicles in an incessant stream. Looking upwards I saw close to me Charing Cross (or *Anglicé* Charing +) railway bridge, breathing smoke from the trains that keep passing over on several lines of metal, with a noise of distant thunder coming through the lattice-work that encloses the level of the bridge. Then, on the same side, beyond Westminster Bridge, the pinnacles and gilded summits of the roofs of the Houses of Parliament nailed themselves to the sky, now getting dusk with evening.

'Does not it seem to you that this gives you an impression of the East?' asked my companion of me.

Just at this moment I was steadily regarding the opposite bank, where beyond the river, with its colour of fuller's earth, with its laden barges, and its long steamers crowded with passengers, there arose two slender towers like Arab minarets: these were towers for the manufacture of small shot.

But close too, on this side, crouching down near to the river, humorously smiled the two sphinxes by the sides of Cleopatra's Needle, the latter placed on a base of bronze. In effect the view lent itself to some indefinite notion of the East. I do not know if it was of India, as I asked my companion, or whether of Egypt, as the sphinxes suggested to me; but perhaps, in virtue of the ideas with which I came, from Assyria or Babylonia, in the colossal times of Sargon or Assurbani-pal. At night I dreamt I was in Nineveh; perhaps because before going to bed, as the moon was magnificently bright, the Thames appeared like a carpet of fishes' scales of burnished steel; the bridge like a constant repetition of flashes followed by thunder; and the lights of the illuminated city, and the gilded summits of Westminster, with the silver-dotted sheet of sky in the background, filled me with the idea of the sight of the pictures that Turner painted, in curious lights, of the ruins of the burned city of the Euphrates.

I put aside the great modern Babylon, and there came to my ears the gigantic hum of millions of human beings, who go out of their way to agitate themselves with the painful murmur implied in a life by ourselves made up of toils and troubles, while Nature, kind and simple, has portioned it out to us as calm and easy.

I heard the gigantic palpitation, the dull thunder, of these twenty thousand streets of London that measure three thousand miles, and give access to nine hundred thousand houses, and carry streams of people along them in more than ten thousand cabs, besides a thousand tramway-cars, two thousand omnibuses, and local railways, including the Underground, that goes under the streets. Of drivers and conductors alone there is an army of thirty thousand men. In the City alone, the kernel of the immense fruit called London, grown with the substance of the whole world – in the City alone, there go daily in and out, except on Sundays, ninety thousand vehicles and more than a million people. Within a radius of six or seven miles from Charing Cross, there are within the circumference of London more than two hundred miles of rail in operation.

London is the double of Paris, the triple of Berlin, nearly the quadruple of Vienna or New York, the quintuple of St. Petersburg, more than ten times the size of Madrid, and fifteen times as large as Rome and Copenhagen. It has more Catholics than Rome, more Jews than all Palestine, more Scotch than Aberdeen, more Welsh than Cardiff, and more Irish than Belfast.

Oliveira Martins, 1894

A glance at Shaftesbury Avenue or the Charing Cross Road will show that London has little talent for lining its new streets with buildings of grandeur, or even dignity. In the case of the Victoria Embankment success was achieved, but has of course since been thrown away. The white Savoy Hotel, where Oliveira Martins stayed, is a rare survivor among the original buildings.

HOW TO SEE ST. PAUL'S

Where the young man stood, if he looked down the river he could see, close at hand, Southwark Bridge, and, beyond it, the ugly Railway Bridge running into the ugly Railway Station: both together shut out the view of all that lay beyond – London Bridge and the Tower and the masts of the ships in the Pool. Even the most splendid sunset cannot make the Cannon Street Terminus beautiful. But if he looked up the river he saw, first, Blackfriars Bridge, standing out with sharp, clear lines, as if cut out of black cardboard; above it, the dazzling golden light of the western sky; and below it, the broad bosom of the river at the flood. The waters of the river, which under the grey sky of a cloudy day are as brown as the waters of the Arno, and even under the bluest sky of midday lack the brightness of the Tyne and the sparkle of the Usk, now reflected back the wonders of the evening, and were themselves as splendid as the skies above. Then he looked across the river. Immediately opposite rose the pile of St. Paul's, vast and majestic – Bank Side is now the only place where you have a really good view of St. Paul's. On either side of St. Paul's rose in lesser glory the spire of St. Bride, the Dragon of Bow, the pinnacles of Aldermarie, the Tower of St. Michael's, and I know not how many more of Wren's masterpieces; for though the Great Fire destroyed many Churches which were not rebuilt, and though modern barbarians have pulled down many more, London is still a City of Churches, and there are plenty left for those who, when the Great Return takes place and the merchants once more go back to live within the City walls, will look to worship in the old Churches after the manner of their forefathers. Below the Churches, on the northern bank, are the wharves and warehouses – Paul's Wharf, Baynard's Castle, and the ancient Port of Queenhithe. This old harbour still retaineth its former shape, though its buildings, which were once low, mean, and ugly, yet picturesque, have long since

been transformed into others, bigger and uglier, yet not picturesque, and even its old Church with the Golden Ship has been wickedly destroyed by the modern barbarians aforesaid.

Below him, floating bravely on the flood, were moored the broad barges which now, for their number and their goodliness, make the glory of Bank Side. Not one or two are here, but fifty or sixty or a hundred, if you were to count, all of generous tonnage and capacity not to be guessed. There were, this evening, so many of them that they extended even more than halfway across the river. Some had masts and brown canvas sails, now furled, ready to drop down as far as the Nore, if necessary: all were painted gaily with streaks of red, blue, yellow and green: some were empty and waiting for their freight: some were laden, and these seemed to be carrying away all the worthless jetsam of the City.

And on all these things alike – for the sun, whether the sun in Splendour, or the sun at his setting, knows no differences and hath no favourites – on the Dome and upper windows and the Ball and Cross of Paul's, on the Dragon of Bow, on the spires and weathercocks and chimney-pots: on the warehouses, which in the white light of noon make but a dingy show, on the clumsy barges with their brown sails, lay the splendour of the sunset, so that all was illuminated and transformed: the spires were flames of fire: the Towers belonged to some Castle of Phantasy: the warehouses were of precious marble, all purple and crimson, or veined and streaked with colour, grander than any palaces of Venice: the barges were ships of fairyland: and the river, reflecting the glory of the sky, rolled along in a broad and glowing flood finer even than the Grande Canale when the Italian sunset lies upon its waters and paints its marble stairs. For the sun of Italy is not so soft, and under the sky of Italy there lack the mists which in England assume such depth and charm of colour.

Sir Walter Besant, 1889

The fine view of St Paul's from the South Bank described by Walter Besant in 1889 had changed very little when this photograph was taken c. 1907.

The statue of Queen Anne rescued by Augustus Hare (and still to be seen at St Leonards-on-Sea) was Francis Bird's 1712 original. This photograph shows the feeble copy by Richard Belt that replaced it in 1886.

DRAMATIC RESCUE OF A QUEEN

August 16, 1894. – The natural beauty of the garden here is a never-failing delight to me. Most people seem to be so full of expectations from the future that they do not allow themselves to enjoy the present; but when I am at home, I am sure that is not the case with me. On the prettiest site in the grounds I have just finished putting up the statues of Queen Anne and her four satellites by Bird, which formerly stood in front of St. Paul's. They were taken away four years ago, and disappeared altogether till last spring, when my friend Lewis Gilbertson discovered them in a stone-mason's yard on the point of being broken up for the sake of the marble. I found they belonged to three people – the Archbishop of Canterbury, the Bishop of London, and the Lord Mayor, and all these were persuaded to resign their claims to me. The statues were brought down to Holmhurst at great expense, and put up, at much greater, on a home-made pedestal like their old one; and now I hope they are enjoying the verdure and sea-breezes after the smoke of the City.

Augustus J. C. Hare, 1894

THE MAN IN THE MONUMENT

Wandering along Great Tower Street, – and Eastcheap, reminiscent of Falstaff and Dame Quickly, – we reach the ever-fishy region of the Monument. The Monument is so tall that it is difficult to see it; indeed, I cannot tell exactly why the Monument seems always as difficult of discovery as the middle of a maze; you seem continually close upon it, and yet you hardly ever reach it. No one can ever direct the pedestrian to it; though this, indeed, may not be the fault of the Monument, but simply because the average Londoner never does know anything about the immediate neighbourhood he inhabits. He has even been known to live in the next street to the British Museum for years, and then be ignorant that such an institution exists. Such superiority to external facts is, no doubt, noble; but it has its drawbacks. And sometimes the individuals questioned take refuge in a crushing silence. The last time, indeed, that I myself visited the Monument, I inquired politely of two fishy youths in turn of its whereabouts, and received no answer. Possibly this was merely their courteous way of informing me that they were really too busy to attend to such trivialities. To return, however, to the deluding Monument: Dickens, it is true, in *Martin Chuzzlewit* makes Mr. Tom Pinch and Miss Pecksniff find their way thither (Tom, having lost his way, very naturally finds himself at the Monument):

> Coming close below the pillar, it was a great encouragement to Tom to find that the Man in the Monument had simple tastes; that stony and artificial as his residence was, he still preserved some rustic recollections; that he liked plants, hung up bird-cages, was not wholly cut off from fresh groundsel, and kept young trees in tubs. The Man in the Monument was sitting outside his own door, the Monument door; and was actually yawning, as if there were no Monument to stop his mouth, and give him a perpetual interest in his own existence. . . . Two people came to see the Monument, a gentleman and lady; and the gentleman said, "How much a-piece?"
>
> The Man in the Monument replied, "A Tanner."
>
> It seemed a low expression, compared with the Monument.
>
> The gentleman put a shilling into his hand, and the Man in the Monument opened a dark little door. When the gentleman and lady had passed out of view, he shut it again, and came slowly back to his chair.
>
> He sat down and laughed.
>
> "They don't know what a many steps there is!" he said. "It's worth twice the money to stop here. Oh, my eye!"
>
> The Man in the Monument was a Cynic. . . .

The charge for the Monument is (I may remark *en passant*), now changed from a 'tanner' to the humble threepence. (Its summit gallery is now closed in, because of the disagreeable mania for committing suicide from it.) The original inscription on its pedestal, now effaced, was a curious relic of

One of the successors to Dickens's man in the monument seen at his post in the late 1880s. The more reasonable threepence was charged for admission at least as late as 1930, but by 1950 the price was a tanner once more. It is now £1.50.

religious intolerance; showing, by its absurd reference to the 'horrid plott' of 'the Popish factio', the barbarous and primitive state of popular feeling as late as 1681. Wherefore it was that, as Pope said:

> '. . . London's Column, pointing to the skies,
> Like a tall bully, lifts its head and lies.'

Mrs E. T. Cook, 1902

LONDON'S RESPECT FOR ITS ANTIQUITIES

My profoundest and distinctest impression of Phyllidian service is from a delightful lunch which I had one golden noonday in that famous and beautiful house, Crosby Place, Bishopsgate, which remains of much the perpendicular Gothic state in which Sir John Crosby proudly built it from his grocer's and woolman's gains in 1466. It had afterwards added to it the glory of lodging Richard III. I do not know how long it has been an eating-house, but I hope it may long remain so, for the sensation and refreshment of Americans who love a simple and good refection in a medieval setting, at a cost so moderate that they must ever

afterwards blush for it. You penetrate to its innermost perpendicularity through a passage that enclosed a 'quick-lunch' counter, and climb from a most noble banquet-hall crammed with hundreds of mercantile gentlemen 'feeding like one' at innumerable little tables, to a gallery where the musicians must have sat of old. There it was that Phyllis found and neat-handedly served my friend and me, gently experiencing a certain difficulty in our combined addition, but mastering the arithmetical problem presently, and taking our tip with an air of surprise which it never created in any of the English-learning Swiss, French, or Italian Strephons who elsewhere ministered to us.

The waitresses at Crosby Place were of a girlish dignity which never expected and was never visibly offered the familiar pleasantries which are the portion of that strange, sad, English creation, the barmaid. In tens of thousands of London public-houses she stands with her hand on beer-pumps, and exchanges jocose banalities with persons beyond the counter in whose dim regard she must show a mere blur of hardened loveliness against her background of bottles and decanters; but the waitress at Crosby Place is of an ideal behavior as fine as that of any Phyllis in a White Mountain hotel; and I thought it to the honor of the lunchers that they seemed all to know it.

William Dean Howells, 1905

Crosby Hall in Bishopsgate, where William Dean Howells dined so happily in 1904, as it appeared in June 1907. Howells had a table in the gallery that can be seen at the far end of the banqueting hall.

In July, 1907, Crosby Hall ceased to be used as a restaurant, and a few months later, in spite of efforts for its preservation which had the countenance of the King and the Government, it was taken down. So difficult is it for the richest city in the world to keep the few relics of ancient days which have survived! A guarantee fund was raised, but the few thousands more that were required were not forthcoming, and the City tamely allowed its most interesting piece of domestic architecture to be taken down. Arrangements were made by the London County Council for its re-erection as a university hall of residence on land adjoining More House at Chelsea, with the stipulation that the public also should enjoy access to it. No more suitable site could have been chosen, for Crosby House was once the habitation of Sir Thomas More, who is the *genius loci* of Chelsea; but an ancient building cannot be taken to pieces and rebuilt elsewhere without losing the greater part of its interest and charm, and its rebuilding can be regarded as little more than an anodyne for an uneasy conscience.

W. W. Hutchings, 1909

A LOST TREASURE

We unexpectedly entered by a quaint nook from Bishopsgate Street to the church of St. Ethelburga, which has a claim to the New-Yorker's interest from the picturesque fact that Henry Hudson and his ship's company made their communion in it the night before he sailed away to give his name to the lordliest, if not the longest of our rivers, and to help the Dutch found the Tammany régime, which still flourishes at the Hudson's mouth. The comprehensive Cunningham makes no mention of the fact, but I do not know why my genealogist should have had the misgiving which he expressed within the overhearing of the eager pew-opener attending us. She promptly set him right. 'Oh, 'e did *mike* it 'ere, sir. They've been and searched the records,' she said, so that the reader now has it on the best authority.

I wish I could share with him, as easily as this assurance, the sentiment of the quaint place, with its traces of Early English architecture, and its look of being chopped in two; its intense quiet and remoteness in the heart of the city, with the slop-pail of its pew-opener mingling a cleansing odor with the ancient smells which pervade all old churches. But these things are of the nerves and may not be imparted, though they may be intimated.

William Dean Howells, 1905

HOW TO AVOID THE UNWASHED

What Londoner has not, from earliest childhood, been acquainted with the Tower? In the Christmas holidays it presented, as a 'treat', rival attractions with Madame Tussaud's and the 'Zoo'. When not presented under the too-informing care of over-zealous pastors and masters, – when not imbibed

St Ethelburga's as it appeared at the time of the visit by William Dean Howells. The entrance was made slightly less obscure by the removal of the shops in 1932. After surviving centuries of fires and wars and improvements the little church fell a victim to terrorism in 1993.

as too flagrant material for that fly-in-the-ointment, a holiday task, – when not made, in a word, too suggestive of the unpleasant, but necessary paths of learning, – it offered great fascinations to the youthful mind. The warders, in their picturesque 'Beefeater' dress, were ever an unfailing joy; the surprise, indeed, with which I first saw one of these mighty beings descend from his pedestal, and deign to hold simple conversation with ordinary mortals, is still fresh in my memory. Then, the towers and dark passages, up which one could run and clatter joyfully, with all the entrancing and horrid possibility of meeting somebody's headless ghost; the attractive thumbscrew, model of the rack, and headsman's mask, all so appealing to the innocent brutality of childhood; the very wooden and highly coloured 'Queen Elizabeth', riding in full dress, with a page, to Tilbury Fort; the stiff effigies of the mail-clad soldiers, in rows inside the White Tower, – the live soldiers drilling in the sun-lit square outside; – the inspiring music of the band, the roll of the drum, the flocks of wheeling pigeons; how charming it all was!

In the Tower precincts, – if you are careful not to choose a Monday or Saturday, which are free days, for your visit – you may enjoy yourself in your own way and to your heart's content. The warders, – old soldiers, – are pleasant and unobtrusive people, with manners of really wonderful

'And it was on this very spot, ladies and gentleman . . .'. A Yeoman Warder introduces a party of tourists to the gruesome delights of Tower Green, c. 1895.

urbanity, considering the very mixed, and generally unwashed, character, of a large portion of their public. The Tower, apart from the charm of its lurid and romantic history, is a picturesque place. In winter, it is somewhat exposed to the elements, and in summer, owing to its proximity to the Temple of the Fisheries, it is, perhaps, a trifle odoriferous; but on a fine spring or autumn morning, – a spring morning uncursed by east wind, an autumn morning undimmed by river-mist, – you will realise all the beauty, as well as the interest, of the place. Part of its attraction lies in the fact that it is neither a ruin nor a fossil; it is a living place still, and serves for use as well as for show. In old days by turn palace, state prison, inquisition, and 'oubliette', it is now a barrack and government arsenal. Its threatening ring of walled towers, witnesses of so many scenes of blood and cruelty, re-echo now to the merry voices of little School-Board boys, playing foot-ball in the drained and levelled moat below; its paved courts and gravelled enclosures still ring to the tramp of soldiers' feet, but soldiers of a newer and a more humane era.

Mrs. E. T. Cook, 1902

THE LORD MAYOR'S MOB

A week ago, the morning was more foggy. Maud and I went to the Arts and Crafts. (How well I remember the grimly askance-looking old lady in the train, as we went up: glaring at us sideways, with grim drawing-down of mouth-corners.) Fog, whilst at the gallery; so that I, shortsighted, couldn't see Ford Madox Brown's cartoon – 'The Baptism of Edwin'. Coming home, we got caught in the crowds of the Lord Mayor's show. Jammed in helplessly, for a quarter-of-an-hour or more, against the inner railings of Hungerford Bridge. Some of the crowd crowded by: – working men mostly. Strangely, I heard no 'strong language': all rather good-tempered, excepting when the policemen appeared up some side-steps, bidding the folk 'Move along, some of you.' 'That's what we wants to do, as much as you wants us to' &c. &c. I feared M. would get hurt, and put out my hand to shove. 'All right sir! I'll see the lady don't get hurt!' says an old chap; and somehow actually did, all the time he was passing, keep a good six inches' clear space. One man, inside the railway railings close to us, very loud in exhorting the people *not* to crowd: 'there's women and children fainting by

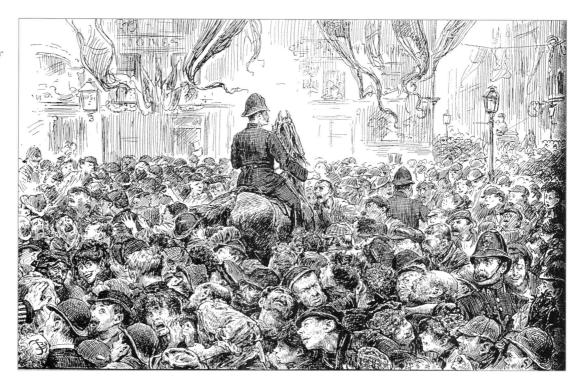

The fearful mob on the rampage during the Lord Mayor's show of 1893, with only the tall figures of the policemen standing out as beacons of sanity and safety.

the score further on! – you're killin' em! women bein' trampled on and killed!' &c. &c. The fellows looked up and let him talk. I heard a baby wailing: and the thing began to look nasty enough: until the bobbies collared some half-dozen fools who were shoving, and sent them with a shove and a kick head first down the stairs. How the 'socialists' would have talked of the 'brutal police'! But I felt some sort of pleasure in seeing this prompt poetic justice. The thing rapidly cleared after that.

George Sturt, 1890

SHRINKING GUARDSMEN

The movement of troops in London from one point to another is one of the evidences of state which is so little static, so largely dynamic. It is a pretty sight, and makes one wish one were a child that one might fully enjoy it, whether it is the movement of a great mass of blood-red backs of men, or here and there a flaming squad, or a single vidette spurring on some swift errand, with his pennoned lance erect from his toe and his horse-hair crest streaming behind him. The soldiers always lend a brilliancy to the

The statuesque sentries at the Horse Guards, one of the unchanging sights of tourist London, are seen here shortly before the Great War.

dull hue of civil life, and there is a never-failing sensation in the spectator as they pass afar or near. Of course, the supreme attraction in their sort for the newly arrived American is the pair of statuesque warriors who motionlessly sit their motionless steeds at the gate of the Horse-Guards, and express an archaic uselessness as perfectly as if they were Highlanders taking snuff before a tobacconist's shop. When I first arrived in London in the earliest of those sad eighteen-sixties when our English brethren were equipping our Confederate brethren to sweep our commerce from the seas, I think I must have gone to see those images at the Horse-Guards even before I visited the monuments in Westminster Abbey, and they then perfectly filled my vast expectation; they might have been Gog and Magog, for their gigantic stature. In after visits, though I had a sneaking desire to see them again, I somehow could not find their place, being ashamed to ask for it, in my hope of happening on it, and I had formed the notion, which I confidently urged, that they had been taken down, like the Wellington statue from the arch. But the other day (or month, rather), when I was looking for Whitehall, suddenly there they were again, sitting their horses in the gateways as of yore, and as woodenly as if they had never stirred since 1861. They were unchanged in attitude, but how changed they were in person: so dwarfed, so shrunken, as if the intervening years had sapped the juices of their joints and let their bones fall together, like those of withered old men!

William Dean Howells, 1905

THE GOTHS

The great argument for Gothic, the great argument, that is, with the general public, who were unable to understand aesthetic considerations, was of course that Gothic was the style of our forefathers, the style in which all the great buildings before the Reformation had been designed and carried out. The cathedrals and the castles were alike adduced, and I think that if another Wren had offered his services, if the native style had been used and carried forward, so to speak, we might have seen a Queen Victoria age of architecture to rival worthily the reign of Queen Anne. But the few Gothic architects who succeeded in the competitions wholly failed to see this. They have left us examples of their powers. We can conclude now with an easy conscience that there was not a Wren among them, not even a Kent or a Burlington. Where they got their way, they showed themselves incapable of using English Gothic to advantage, or they tried for originality and wandered outside the limits of the style; or, worse than all the rest, they designed buildings not in English Gothic at all but in the feeble Gothic of Italy – for which there was not any argument to be found which would appeal to the general public or, indeed, to any one of practical views, not to say of common sense.

The principal examples of the London Gothic of the

The Foreign Office in Exile might be the alternative name for the Midland Grand Hotel at St Pancras station, for it was here that the thrifty George Gilbert Scott used up the Gothic design with which Lord Palmerston would not allow him to pollute Whitehall.

second half of the nineteenth century are enough to prove this abundantly. Scott was appointed to design the new Foreign Office. Lord Palmerston, with his usual good sense, would not have the architect's design. We now know why; and though then the Prime Minister had to endure some very disagreeable language from the architect and his supporters, he was more than justified, because he considered that a very weak imitation of a building in Italian Gothic was not suited to the situation. If it is true that the hotel and railway station at St Pancras are on the lines of the building Scott designed for the street of Whitehall, Lord Palmerston was abundantly justified by the result.

William John Loftie, 1914

AMPLE RECOMPENSE

The frontage of St. Pancras on the Euston Road is one of the finest buildings in London. Designed by Sir Gilbert Scott, it rears its immense mass, built at an expense that has never been reckoned, where once stood slums filthy and innumerable. Underneath the passenger station is another for stores, and underneath that runs yet another railway. Few people walking along the upper platform realise that sixty feet below them is a signal box! The difficulties in constructing this three-storied station were enormous. The whole area covered by the stations is some twenty-five acres, while the span covers nearly 220,000 square feet, and is roughly 100 feet high; the biggest span, until recently, in the world. It is worth while to wander up the Pancras Road at night; the weird and beautiful effects to be seen outside the station amply recompense one for the unpleasant neighbourhood.

Frederick T. Jane, 1893

THE IMPERIAL ZOO

Even at such a place as the Zoological Gardens, which they must have been visiting all their lives, there were, at least, a thousand Englishmen for every cultivated American we could make sure of when we went there; and as it was a Sunday, when the gardens are closed to the general public, this overwhelming majority of natives must have come on orders from Fellows of the Society such as we had supposed would admit us much more selectly, if not solely. Still, the place was not crowded, and if it had been, still it would have been delightful on a summer afternoon, of that hovering softness, half-cloud, half-sun, which the London sky has the patent of. The hawthorn-trees, white and pink with their may, were like cloudlets dropped from that sky, as it then was and would be at sunset; and there was a density of grass underfoot and foliage overhead in which one's own childhood found itself again, so that one felt as free for the simple pleasure of consorting with strange beasts and birds as if one were still ten or eleven years old. But I cannot hope to rejuvenate my readers in the same degree, and so had better not insist upon the animals; the herds of elephants, the troops of lions and tigers, the schools of hippopotamuses, and the mass-meetings of anthropoid apes. Above and beyond these in their strangeness were the figures of humanity representative of the globe-girdling British empire, in their drawers and turbans and their swarthy skins, who could urge a patriotic interest, impossible for me, in the place. One is, of course, used to all sorts of alien shapes in Central Park, but there they are somehow at once less surprising and less significant than these Asian and African forms; they will presently be Americans, and like the rest of us; but those dark imperialings were already British and eternally un-English. They frequented the tea-tables spread in pleasant shades and shelters, and ate buns and bread-and-butter, like their fellow-subjects, but their dark liquid eyes roamed over the blue and gold and pink of the English complexions with an effect of mystery irreconcilable forever with the matter-of-fact mind behind their bland masks. We

The undisputed star of the zoo during the 1895 season was the new giraffe, which 'has submitted with the best of grace to the inevitable interviewer, and has posed most excellently' for a continuous procession of artists.

called them Burmese, Eurasians, Hindoos, Malays, and fatigued ourselves with guessing at them so that we were faint for the tea from which they kept us at the crowded tables in the gardens or on the verandas of the tea-houses. But we were not so insatiable of them as of their fellow-subjects, the native British whom one sees at a Sunday of the Zoo to perhaps special advantage. Our Sunday was in the season, and the season had conjecturably qualified it, so that one could sometimes feel oneself in company better than one's own. The children were well-dressed and admirably well-behaved; they justly outnumbered their elders, and it was obviously their day. But it was also the day of their elders, who had made excuse of the children's pleasure in coming to the Zoo for their own. Some indeed were not so much their elders, and the young aunts and uncles, who were naturally cousins, lost themselves at times a little way from the children and maids, in the quieter walks or nooks, or took boat to be alone on the tranquil waters with one another. They were then more interesting than the strangest Malays and Hindoos, and I wonder what these made of them, as they contemplated their segregation with the other thronging spectators.

William Dean Howells, 1905

L.C.C. STEAMBOATS ARRIVE . . .

Strangers were admitted on the rigid terms and in the strict limits to which non-members must submit themselves. But one might well undergo much more in order to hear John Burns speak in the place to which he has fought his right under a system of things as averse as can be imagined to a working-man's sharing in the legislation for working-men. The matter in hand that night chanced to be one peculiarly interesting to a believer in the people's doing as many things as possible for themselves, as the body politic, instead of leaving them to a variety of bodies corporate. The steamboat service on the Thames had grown so insufficient and so inconvenient that it was now a question of having it performed by the London County Council, which should be authorized to run lines of boats solely in the public interest, and not merely for the pleasure and profit of directors and stockholders. The monstrous proposition did not alarm those fears of socialism which anything of the kind would have roused with us; nobody seemed to expect that blowing up the Parliament

The London County Council's steamboat Rennie *doing good business at Lambeth Pier in August 1907, shortly before the service was withdrawn.*

buildings with dynamite would be the next step towards anarchy. There was a good deal of hear-hearing from Mr. Burns's friends, with some friendly chaffing from his enemies as he went on, steadily and quietly, with his statement of the case; but there was no serious opposition to the measure which was afterwards carried in due course of legislation.

Several members spoke besides Mr. Burns, but the labor leader was easily first, not only in the business quality of what he said, but in his business fashion of saying it. As much as any of them, as the oldest-familied and longest-leisured of them, his manners had

'that repose
Which marks the caste of Vere de Vere,'

and is supposed to distinguish them from those of the castes of Smith and Brown. But I quickly forgot this in considering how far socialism had got itself realized in London through the activities of the County Council, which are so largely in the direction of municipal control. One hears and reads as little of socialism now in London as in New York, but that is because it has so effectually passed from the debated principle to the accomplished fact.

William Dean Howells, 1905

. . . AND DEPART

The steamboats run by private enterprise in the second decade of the nineteenth century at first did well, but presently the service degenerated, and at last in 1905, having greatly improved the old piers, and provided new ones, the London County Council came to the rescue with a municipal steamboat service. Some of the boats were kept running during the winter of that year as an experiment, but in the next year the winter service was abandoned, and after the end of the following summer season the service was discontinued, for the ratepayers had a spasm of economy, and the boats, although during that last season they had carried more than two and a-quarter million passengers, had not proved to be self-supporting. Perhaps London may some day make up its mind to regard the question from another than the strict profit-and-loss point of view, and, with the consent of both the parties in municipal politics, may be content to regard the few thousand pounds a year which the service would cost the ratepayers as having an ample return in the pleasure which it would yield to hundreds of thousands of the people.

W. W. Hutchings, 1909

Chapter 4

ENTERTAINMENTS

In a world before wireless and television, and where the cinema was still only a comical infant, the theatre was the king of London entertainment. With nearly the whole population to satisfy, it naturally took many forms. For the common people there were music hall and rousing melodrama, in which a ferocious hound frequently provided the climax. The villain 'concealed a nice juicy piece of uncooked meat round his neck, and at the critical moment, to the music of a full orchestra, the dog fastened his teeth into the meat; the man and he struggled all over the stage. The realism of the combat brought the house down, and the villain and the curtain simultaneously. That was something like a drama!'

For the hypocritical, nonconformist middle classes there was a theatre that pretended not to be a theatre. At the St George's Hall in Langham Place the German Reed dynasty provided a mixture of dramatic scenes and musical interludes that allowed the puritanical to enjoy the thrills of the play and the music hall (but with the sex left out), while still being able to claim that they had never set foot in a theatre. The less severe patronised the Lyceum or Her Majesty's, where Irving and his young rival Tree staged their spectacular pageants, or Drury Lane, 'our National Theatre', where the great attraction was the pantomime. For a sophisticated West End audience George Alexander, 'the matinée idol *par excellence*', produced the works of Wilde and Pinero at the St James's,

while the Independent Theatre presented Ibsen and Shaw for the avant-garde.

Covent Garden, the home of the Royal Italian Opera (and the occasional circus), had no serious rival, although ill-fated attempts to challenge its far from profitable monopoly were made by Richard D'Oyly Carte in 1891, with the Royal English Opera House, now the Palace Theatre, and by Oscar Hammerstein in 1911 at the London Opera House in Kingsway. The Royal Albert Hall and the Crystal Palace were the two largest concert halls, but both tended to offer more dog shows and political rallies than symphonies and oratorios. Exeter Hall in the Strand, long a famous venue for the best music, had been lost to the YMCA in 1880 (and was demolished in 1907), but the opening of the Queen's Hall in 1893 was more than adequate compensation.

Sport was being increasingly taken up by the working classes and becoming professional in the process. It was still the fashion to speak of the two forms of football as being of equal prominence, but soccer had long outstripped rugby and was now challenging the ancient supremacy of cricket. Tennis and golf began their great rise to favour, cycling and skating came and went, and indoors 'the tyranny of bridge' had begun. This was an age in which every kind of sport was being organised and codified after an infancy of haphazard amateur development and eccentric local rules.

Scotland outplayed England in the rugby match at Richmond on 7 March 1891, and triumphed by 3 goals to 1. The sketch probably shows W. Neilson of Merchiston scoring the decisive try.

SIR HENRY

Irving as Mephistopheles produces the most vivid impression possible for a great actor. Grandeur and simplicity, shallows and depths, the charming sweetness of the homely scene, the divinely terrific beauty of the supernatural episode – he represents them all with marvellous ease, with admirable certainty. While entering into the identity of his part, he develops it with a tact and an intelligence of which no other player in the world is capable, thereby often producing the most starting effects.

Without bestowing undue praise, all must agree that nowhere has he his equal in the matter of stage scenery. To have any idea of what such an artist and scene producer as Irving can do, one must have seen Marguerite's garden, the walls of Nuremberg, the street near the cathedral, the Brocken. The terrific grandeur of the scene on the Brocken surpasses anything imaginable. What effects of unearthly light; what a terrible storm rends the sky, hurling its thunderbolts upon rocks where demons merrily dance; what colourless, formless spectres glide through the sulphurous atmosphere! Surely such have never before been produced on the boards of any theatre.

Gabriel Mourey, 1895

In 1895, to the delight of the nation, Irving was knighted by Queen Victoria. It was the first time such an honour had ever been conferred upon an actor, and by the address presented to him by four thousand of his brother and sister actors they showed a fitting sense of the importance of the innovation. This was the climax of a great career. The taste for serious drama, even when produced with dazzling splendour, was beginning to decline, and during a protracted illness which overtook Irving in 1898, the Lyceum passed into the hands of a limited liability company, who acquired it for £275,000, and now the Lyceum was available for nine months in the year to almost anyone who elected to hire it. It was finally closed in 1902, owing to inability to comply with the quite proper but very costly structural requirements of the London County Council, and on the 30th of September, 1903, the shareholders, after hearing a letter from Irving deprecating the change, but not opposing it, decided to convert it into a music hall. It then underwent reconstruction, and was reopened as a variety theatre on the 31st of December, 1904. The distinguished man who had won immortal fame upon its boards did not long survive the change: he died suddenly at Bradford on the 13th of October in the following year, at the close of a performance of Becket, and was buried in Westminster Abbey. In April, 1907, the Lyceum was successfully reopened with a melodrama, and since October, 1908, by way of keeping up its reputation for versatility, it has been on Sundays the preaching centre of the West London Mission, the organisation founded by the late Rev. Hugh Price Hughes at St. James's Hall.

W. W. Hutchings, 1909

A portrait of Sir Henry Irving, the great actor whose mannerisms made him a gift to the imitator. His attempt to raise his craft to the dignity of a profession perhaps did it no real favour.

AUGUSTUS DRURIOLANUS

'The Gaiety Bar' was in those days, practically speaking, the literary and artistic Bohemians' club. Before my eyes now I imagine I can see the familiar figure of Gus Harris, with the glossiest of silk hats worn at a perilous angle on one side of his head, his florid complexion, sparkling eyes, and the smile of self-satisfaction that is the heritage of the successful few! I can see him now, as was his wont, strutting up and down the Gaiety Bar, attired in immaculate evening dress with the then fashionable Inverness cape thrown over one shoulder.

'Augustus Druriolanus' was a shrewd, long-sighted, long-headed genius. He was essentially plucky, and for this quality, and for playing the game like a sportsman, he always commanded my sincere admiration.

Harry Furniss, 1919

Drury Lane was the cornerstone of Harris's empire, and the mainstay of Drury Lane was the pantomime, which he raised to unprecedented levels of splendour and spectacle. In 1893 the gods of the gallery were clearly enthralled by his efforts.

Augustus Harris was a hearty, genial man with a bluff and boisterous manner, but on occasions he could wrap himself in a cloak of dignity.

Once in the long ago, when Arthur Pinero was just beginning to come to the front, there was a theatrical dinner at the Star and Garter, Richmond, with a large professional attendance and speeches afterwards.

Pinero made a little speech, and something he said quite innocently was taken by Harris to reflect on the policy at Drury Lane. When the company filed out after the banquet Gus Harris planted himself in the doorway and waited until Pinero came along. Then he eyed him up and down in the good old melodramatic manner and exclaimed:

'Mushroom!'

Some years afterwards Arthur Pinero had made his mark, and a very big mark, as a dramatic author, and he found himself at the Green Room Club late one night when Augustus Harris was there.

Several of the members remembered that since the dinner the manager and author had not spoken to each other.

One of them – I think it was Henry Hamilton – went to Gus and said, 'Come and speak to Pinero. What's the good of nursing an old grievance?'

Harris had his cloak on – a sort of military cloak which he generally wore over evening dress. Presently, after evident hesitation, he strode towards Pinero, flung the folds of his cloak over his shoulder, looked the now successful author up and down, and exclaimed:

*Sir Augustus Harris (1852–96), the great London theatrical
impresario, as affectionately caricatured by Harry Furniss.*

'Shakespeare!'

I think Druriolanus imagined that he had both offended
and atoned monosyllabically, because when he and Pettitt
were discussing the title for a new play Harris said, 'What
I like best are monosyllabic titles like *Humanity.*'

George R. Sims, 1917

CARTHAGE IN THE HAYMARKET

For some months past there has been a ruin at the corner of
the Haymarket, westward of Waterloo Place. The dilapidated
edifice occupied a vast space of ground, at the eastern side of
the Haymarket, and extending north and south from Charles
Street to Pall Mall. It used to be known as Her Majesty's
Theatre, but I prefer to call it Carthage, for the reasons of the
infinite wretchedness of its plight and of the famous
memories which it recalls. With our usual impatience of
ruins, however, on its being generally confessed that there
was no chance of prosperity for Her Majesty's Theatre as a
home of Italian Opera, or, indeed, as a place devoted to any
other kind of entertainment, and the Crown lease having
fallen in, the theatre was not allowed slowly to subside into
ruins, but was deliberately and ferociously torn down, with
the view of straightway erecting a structure of quite another
character in its place.

It does not in the least matter to me whether the new
edifice which is to arise on the area of the Haymarket

Carthage is to be a Co-operative Store, or a branch of the
General Post-Office, or a Brobdingnagian bucket shop, or
another West-End branch of the Sempiternal Wild Cat Bank,
Unlimited, or a gigantic hotel. I have heard that the last
named is to be its destiny; but I prefer to regard it only as a
congener of the antique African city which was set on fire by
the Romans, and burned incessantly during seventeen days;
which was partially rebuilt by Augustus, wrested from the
Romans by Genseric and his Vandals, and at last fell into
the hands of the Saracens. Do you know Tasso's lines on the
delended city? I will give them to you as beautifully rendered
by Fairfax:

> Great Carthage low in ashes cold doth lie,
> Her ruins poor, the herbs in height scant pass;
> So cities fall, so perish kingdoms high,
> Their pride and pomp lie hid in sand and grass.

I repeated these lines to myself the last time when, coming
from Pall Mall, I turned to behold the Opera Colonnade, the
pillars smeared over with colours once garish, now dirty, and
branded with the inscriptions of 'Lot 54', 'Lot 107', and so
forth, and saw that the façade of the once splendid theatre
had been wholly demolished, the auditorium entirely
dismantled, the stage ripped up, and only something like the
phantoms of the frame of the proscenium, and of the
different tiers of boxes remaining in unsightly brickwork.
Where were the yellow satin curtains; where the huge central
chandelier; and where, oh! where, the scenery and the
costumes, the decorations, and, more than all, the wondrous
harmonies, vocal and instrumental, that once made the Italian
Opera House one of the chief glories of London? All gone as
thoroughly and as hopelessly as Dido's city, the building of
which was painted with such wondrous exuberance of
imagination by our Turner. Would that he were alive to paint
Carthage in the Haymarket by moonlight, and Colonel
Mapleson musing like Marius of old among its ruins!

George Augustus Sala, 1894

A SHOCK OF SURPRISE

To see Tree make up for his part was a privilege I often
enjoyed. There in his dressing-room you saw the artist at work,
the creative artist who adds touch after touch to complete the
picture, until suddenly the whole conception bursts into
significant life. When Tree had thoroughly got inside the skin
of a character – which often took some time – he seemed to
partake of a new and alien life. A singular illustration was
Zakkuri in the *Darling of the Gods*, in which by degrees Tree
gave us, I do not say a true, but an extraordinarily vivid and
convincing portrait of a Japanese statesman in all his horrible
subtlety and coarseness. Another example was Izard in *Business
is Business*. Tree was never a smoker in the true sense of the
word; he only smoked for the sake of companionship, taking a
modest fourpenny cigar, while he gave his guest Coronas. But
in Izard he was perpetually smoking big and black-looking

The view up the Haymarket from Pall Mall in 1890, with the old Her Majesty's Theatre on the left. It was demolished in 1891, and replaced by the present Her Majesty's, the creation of Beerbohm Tree, in 1897.

cigars. I asked him how he managed to stand it; he answered that, as it seemed natural to the character, he found it easy for himself. Off the stage he could not have done it; on the stage it was appropriate and therefore a piece of unconscious mimicry. Svengali smoked, I think, cigarettes or long Vevey *fins*. The Duke of Guisebury smoked, quite as to the manner born, a pipe – a luxury in which Tree, the individual, not the actor, never indulged.

He was always unexpected, daring, original; he often gave one a shock of surprise, welcome or unwelcome. He was good when you anticipated a relative failure; poor, when you could have wagered on his success. His acting was never monotonous, rarely the same from night to night. Like his conversation, it was full of quick turns and unlooked-for spurts of vivid, graphic, picturesque, satisfying the eye, even when occasionally he failed to satisfy the mind. When he was acting Mark Antony in the Forum scene he broke off the famous speech in the middle, came down from the rostrum, and finished his speech standing on a broken pillar. I argued with him about this, suggesting that if Mark Antony was really holding his audience he would never have altered his position. Tree answered: 'You forget the soon-wearied eye of the spectator; he becomes tired of one situation and demands another. Besides,' he added, with a whimsical smile, 'change is a necessity for my nature.' It was indeed. And, owing to this he became tired and bored with his part, and sometimes broke off the run of a piece in the midst of a brilliant success! I anticipate what you will say, my critical friend! You will remind me that I am describing the qualities of an amateur, not of a professional. I do not shrink from the conclusion. Tree had all the best points of an amateur, and some of his

Sir Herbert Beerbohm Tree, the master of disguise, made up for the role of Paragot in 'The Beloved Vagabond', a dramatisation of W.J. Locke's 1906 best-seller.

triumphs were gained just for that reason. He was a glorified amateur who dared things which a professional never would have dared, and won a shining victory. He mistrusted all talk about technique. 'I have not got technique,' he once said; 'it is a dull thing. It enslaves the imagination.'

W. L. Courtney, 1917

An 1893 caricature of Albert Chevalier (one of the last great stars of music hall) in his special 'Knocked 'em in the Old Kent Road' costume.

THE SENTIMENTAL COSTER

I write the words of my songs myself. I have a good ear for music – for instance, I can play the fiddle fairly well and the guitar and banjo a little, – and a small part of my music I write myself also, or, rather, I get hold of odd bits and 'fake' them. But even the 'faking' process I do not rely upon much: good music, I am sure, is now most essential in the music-hall. Whether it is that musical education is getting 'forrader', or not, I do not know; but I do know that an audience like decent harmony, and are not content with what I may call the mere 'tum-tum-tum-tune.' My brother writes a great portion of my music – Mr. John Cook wrote the music for 'The Serenade' – then I take pains to have it well arranged, and Mr. Asher, the conductor at the Tivoli, kindly undertakes the arrangement of most of my music for the orchestra.

I suppose, on the whole, 'Knocked 'em in the Old Kent Road' has been my most popular song; but 'The Coster's Serenade', 'The Future Mrs. 'Awkins', 'The Coster's Courtship' have all had their ample meed of success. The song I am giving now, 'My Old Dutch' will open out, I hope, a wider field in front of it and has proved a great catch in the publishing line as well as for acting purposes. For it does not at all follow that a song which is a success as a stage song has a good sale. People may think (and often they are right) that it requires costume and scene to exhibit it to advantage.

The music-hall stage is not all glory and honour, nor pavement of gold. Like every other profession it demands hard work. I, for instance, do four halls every night, and, on Saturdays two *matinées* as well. I begin each night at the Royal in Holborn at about 8.30; about 9.30 I go from there to the Canterbury in Westminster Bridge Road; at 10.30 I am at the Tivoli in the Strand; at 11 o'clock I am due at the Pavilion in Piccadilly Circus. As a rule I sing three songs at each, though I try to get off with two. I used to sing all my songs in one rig-out with the exception of 'The Old Kent Road', and then had only to don a different coat and waistcoat. But now, for 'My Old Dutch', I have to make a change from top to toe, paint and the rest of it, but I can do the whole change in two minutes, and have in fact done it in less. Then back to my original dress – a change I can do in one minute – for my last song, and I am in the right costume also for my first song at the next show, and sometimes I have had to get out of my brougham, on my arrival at the next hall, and walk straight from it on to the stage.

Albert Chevalier, 1893

QUITE INOFFENSIVE

Went to hear Mr Albert Chevalier's Recital. I only knew of him as being *facile princeps* among music-hall singers, and did not remember that I had seen him twice or oftener on the stage – first as 'Mr Hobbs' in 'Little Lord Fauntleroy', and afterwards as a 'horsy' young man in a *matinée* in which Violet Vanbrugh appeared. He was decidedly *good* as an actor; but as a comic singer (with considerable powers of pathos as well) he is quite first-rate. His chief merit seems to be the earnestness with which he throws himself into the work. The songs (mostly his own writing) were quite inoffensive, and very funny. I am very glad to be able to think that his influence on public taste is towards refinement and purity. I liked best 'The Future Mrs 'Awkins', with its taking tune, and 'My Old Dutch', which revealed powers that, I should think, would come out grandly in Robsonian parts, such as 'The Porter's Knot'. 'The Little Nipper' was also well worth hearing.

Lewis Carroll, 1893

A PATRIOTIC FRENZY

Beautiful Rose appears. She dances as other serpentine dancers, but on a golden ball. Magic beams of light flash from its curves. But the audience remain unmoved; they have often seen it before. And though the delicate, subtle tints blend, clothing and reanimating the scene with unexpected and varied splendour, yet the people display no emotion.

At one time showers of golden stars set in a blue background mingle with the dancer's floating drapery; at another, starry flowers, masses of spring petals painted by the brush of dawn – till you dream of Botticelli's *Primavera*. The audience applaud feebly, and resume their stolid indifference. Suddenly a passion of excitement thrills through the hall;

While Albert Chevalier was edging the music hall towards refinement, purity, and extinction, his great contemporary Marie Lloyd (seen here c. 1905) remained true to the racy and vulgar origins of the form. She could sing a hymn in a way that made the Lord Chamberlain itch to ban it.

hurrahs are heard on all sides, for the garments of Beautiful Rose assume the form of British drapery; she dances among the revolving sacrosanct colours. The air is a flood of glory; English patriotism is stirred. The spectators are beside themselves with delight; a delirium of joy seizes them. In turns the portrait of the Duke and Duchess of York appears on the dancer's form, the Duke on the right side, the Duchess on the left. At one time the Prince of Wales, at another the Princess. Then she slackens her speed as if she were giddy. Folds of drapery are fantastically whirled round the poles on which her arms are extended. The Prince of Wales' face dances madly. The whole audience is on foot, stamping, quivering, in a paroxysm of enthusiasm. A cry of joy greets the appearance of the Queen – the Queen herself, with crown on head – while the orchestra plays *God save the Queen*. There is a touch of the fantastic about it. The most decorous among the spectators clap their hands, stamp their feet and utter loud cries of approval. On the dancer's majestic form, which seems transparent under the powerful light of

the brilliant curves, the effigy of her Majesty oscillates, trembles, loses its shape, staggers as if with drunkenness.

Then everything is extinguished, and a great silence reigns. The crisis is over. The fanatics of a minute ago sit down quietly, collectedly, without emotion, and the entertainment continues.

Gabriel Mourey, 1895

PROMS AND PURITANS

Mr. Robert Newman's Queen's Hall Orchestra has a world-wide reputation. Much of its success is due to the personality of its leader, Mr. Henry J. Wood. On the nights when the programme consists mainly of the music of Wagner or Tschaikowsky you will find the handsome hall literally filled from roof to floor with a brilliant audience. The members of the orchestra, who are mostly English, are young, alert, enthusiastic. Mr. Wood takes up his place as conductor. You notice a pale, intellectual face; dark hair worn rather long, and an indefinable suggestion of individuality. From the moment that the music begins you realise that Mr. Wood and his instrumentalists are one harmonious whole. To his every gesture, however slight, the players respond. He obtains the most marvellous effects of light and shade. In Beethoven's C minor Symphony, in the 'Symphonie Pathétique' of Tschaikowsky, in a Serenade for Strings composed by one of the members of his band, or in a French Ballet-Suite, the work of Mr. Wood and his colleagues is ever of the highest excellence.

And, as a proof that it is not merely the wealthier class of musical amateurs who appreciate the value of Mr. Newman's enterprise, witness the crowds who flock to the Queen's Hall on summer evenings what time the Promenade Concerts are in progress. For a shilling you may hear the finest music performed by Mr. Wood's orchestra, and you may walk about and smoke withal.

Gilbert Burgess, 1901

The total destruction of the Queen's Hall, Langham Place, was one of London's irreparable losses of the Second World War. With its perfect acoustics, it immediately captured the leading position in London's musical life when it opened in 1893. It is now especially remembered as the first home of the Henry Wood Proms.

A Conductor for the Deaf

Went to the Queen's Hall, sat in the Orchestra and watched Sir Henry's statuesque figure conducting thro' a forest of bows, 'which pleased me mightily'. He would be worth watching if you were stone deaf. If you could not hear a sound, the animation and excitement of an orchestra in full swing, with the conductor cutting and slashing at invisible foes, make a magnificent spectacle.

The face of Sir Henry Wood strikes me as very much like the traditional pictures of Jesus Christ, tho' Sir Henry is dark – the melanic Messiah I call him (very much to my own delight). Rodin ought to do him in stone – Chesterfield's ideal of a man – a Corinthian edifice on Tuscan foundations. In Sir Henry's case there can be no disputing the Tuscan foundations. However swift and elegant the movements of his arms, his splendid lower extremities remain as firm as stone columns. While the music is calm and serene his right hand and bâton execute, in concert with the left, perfect geometric curves around his head. Then as it gathers in force and volume, when the bows begin to dart swiftly across the fiddles and the trumpets and trombones blaze away in a conflagration, we are all expectant – and even a little fearful, to observe his sabre-like cuts. The tension grows . . . I hold my breath. . . . Sir Henry snatches a second to throw back a lock of his hair that has fallen limply across his forehead, then goes on in unrelenting pursuit, cutting and slashing at hordes of invisible fiends that leap howling out towards him. There is a great turmoil of combat, but the Conductor struggles on till the great explosion happens. But in spite of that, you see him still standing thro' a cloud of great chords, quite undaunted. His sword zigzags up and down the scale – suddenly the closed fist of his left hand shoots up straight and points to the zenith – like the arm of a heathen priest appealing to Baal to bring down fire from Heaven. . . . But the appeal avails nought and it looks as tho' it were all up for poor Sir Henry. The music is just as infuriated – his body writhes with it – the melanic Messiah crucified by the inappeasable desire to express by visible gestures all that he feels in his heart. He surrenders – so you think – he opens out both arms wide and baring his breast, dares them all to do their worst – like the picture of Moffat the missionary among the savages of the Dark Continent!

And yet he wins after all. At the very last moment he seems to summon all his remaining strength and in one final and devastating sweep mows down the orchestra rank by rank. . . . You awake from the nightmare to discover the victor acknowledging the applause in a series of his inimitable bows.

One ought to pack one's ears up with cotton wool at a concert where Sir Henry conducts. Otherwise, the music is apt to distract one's attention.

'W. N. P. Barbellion', 1914

Divine Harmony

Our German friends, who have so considerately left their 'Happy Fatherland' to test the English taste for music, are happily getting less numerous every year, but there are still

The German band, almost as great a nuisance a hundred years ago as the ghetto-blaster of today, as it appeared on the London streets in 1892.

a few left – some tolerable, some otherwise. They are brought over from the agricultural parts of Germany by an enterprising bandmaster, who gives them four shillings a week, pays their fares, provides instruments, uniforms, board and lodging, and teaches them to play some instrument. Their pay increases according to the progress they make. Fulham is their headquarters and Sunday their practice day. The novices begin playing in the northern and eastern suburbs of London, and, as they improve, they are promoted to the south-west and west. A guide goes with them, and he does the collecting. Denmark Hill being a favourite residential locality for well-to-do Germans the best bands generally work – or rather play – that way.

Dogs, especially singing dogs, take great delight in German bands, and may often be seen, with their noses skyward, lifting up their voices in grand chorus, and are no doubt supremely disgusted that their efforts to increase the harmony are not appreciated by the bandsmen.

Gilbert Guerdon, 1892

Travelling at Home

Constantinople at Olympia is a dazzling scene of enchantment and splendour, and exquisite taste; a medley of decorations, costumes, accessories, dancers, acrobats, ballet-girls, and all the excitable people of the East. There are fifteen hundred or two thousand individuals who whirl round, dance, move to and fro, mingle, disperse, crowd together under the light of the electric balls. There are triumphal processions, flourish of trumpets and waving of flags, camels and horses, palanquins and warriors, captives and sultanas, dances, games, pantomimes, clowns. The orchestra seems to play under the water, the brown handles of the contrabasses alone appearing to destroy the illusion, as in certain sketches by Degas. And the big lake reflects it

'Constantinople' (1893/4) was one of a series of spectacular entertainments mounted at Olympia during the 1890s. In other years the stay-at-home could sample the delights of 'The Orient' or experience 'Venice in London'. 1. A Street scene. 2. Entrance to the Hall of the Thousand and One Pillars. 3. Caiques for Hire. 4. Place Stamboul and Rue Pera.

A VIOLENT SPASM OF GENEROSITY

In the carrying out of the Exhibition of 1851, and in the conception and execution of the vast scheme which was its sequel, the late Lord Playfair took a leading part, and to him belongs the credit of initiating the movement for the completion of the Victoria and Albert Museum buildings. They date from 1857, when a temporary structure, mainly of iron, occupying the site of the Architectural Court, was opened. Permanent buildings were soon afterwards begun, and in 1868 the greater part of the temporary structure was taken down. Some extensions were from time to time made, as the collection grew in volume, but from 1884 onwards nothing effectual was done, and in a letter to the *Times* in the year of the Diamond Jubilee Lord Playfair declared the

The South Kensington Museum was housed for more than forty years in a temporary structure like a series of huge Nissen huts, and known derisively as the Brompton Boilers. The Queen renamed it the Victoria and Albert Museum when she laid the foundation stone of Aston Webb's new building in 1899. The photograph was taken at about the time of the official opening in 1909.

all. In its motionless surface and amid its moving mirrors, you may see yourself seated under eastern tents, assisting at the penumbra of the *fête*.

Outside, surrounding the vast hall, are streets of Turkish shops; genuine harems enclosed in glass are seen under arcades of flashing mirrors. Near the bridges lie steamers on the point of departure, and from the orchestra proceed strains of weird music.

There are also on view the port, the quays of Constantinople, with their horizon of mosques and minarets, and the domes of St. Sophia. Boats take you by underground canals to the tiers of columns and mirrors, which multiply and re-multiply indefinitely. Pavilioned harbours entwined with flowers emerge from the water as if they were part of some true 'Arabian Night' story. And while you remain in this fairyland you forget even the spectators around you, who have more the air of inquisitive loafers in a foreign country than of people who have paid their money for a seat at a show.

Gabriel Mourey, 1895

position to be that while the collections were splendid, the accommodation was inadequate and the Museum had no proper setting. "In front of it there are bare brick walls, the 'Brompton boilers', shabby railway vans and sheds, and altogether a general squalor which humiliates the nation in the eyes of foreigners who come in large numbers to visit the Museum." And he suggested that the Government should ask Queen Victoria's permission to change its name from the South Kensington to the Victoria Museum and should take a small supplementary vote towards the commencement of the façade which it so sorely lacked. This suggestion chimed in with the nation's mood. In a violent spasm of generosity Parliament, usually so little regardful of the nation's higher needs, granted not a mere vote on account but a round sum of £800,000, and on the 17th of May, 1899, Queen Victoria laid the foundation-stone of the new buildings and officially declared that for ever afterwards the institution should bear the name of the Victoria and Albert Museum. The new façade, of which Sir Aston Webb, R.A., is the designer, overlooks Cromwell Road, along which it extends for seven hundred feet, and Exhibition Road as far northwards as the Royal College of Science, and it fully doubles the area of the main building. With the re-arrangement of the contents of the Museum which this extension permits the Museum will cease to be the derision of the stranger within our gates. Ruskin has related how, when he once went to the Museum, he lost himself in a labyrinth and had to put himself in charge of a policeman to get out again, and it is on record that when a visitor enquired for a view of the Museum he found none on sale. 'You see, sir,' explained the attendant, 'the Museum doesn't stand still long enough to be photographed.'

W. W. Hutchings, 1909

GREEN PARK – THREE AMERICAN IMPRESSIONS

I have a weakness for the convenient, familiar, treeless, or almost treeless, expanse of the Green Park, and the friendly part it plays as a kind of encouragement to Piccadilly. I am so fond of Piccadilly that I am grateful to any one or anything that does it a service, and nothing is more worthy of appreciation than the southward look it is permitted to enjoy just after it passes Devonshire House – a sweep of horizon which it would be difficult to match among other haunts of men, and thanks to which, of a summer's day, you may spy, beyond the browsed pastures of the foreground and middle distance, beyond the cold chimneys of Buckingham Palace and the towers of Westminster and the swarming river-side and all the southern parishes, the hard modern twinkle of the roof of the Crystal Palace.

Henry James, 1888

Among those who carry the banner, Green Park has the reputation of opening its gates earlier than the other parks, and at quarter-past four in the morning, I, and many more, entered Green Park. It was raining again, but they were worn out with the night's walking, and they were down on the benches and asleep at once. Many of the men stretched out full length on the dripping wet grass, and, with the rain falling steadily upon them, were sleeping the sleep of exhaustion.

And now I wish to criticise the powers that be. They *are* the powers, therefore they may decree whatever they please; so I make bold only to criticise the ridiculousness of their decrees. All night long they make the homeless ones walk up and down. They drive them out of doors and passages, and lock them out of the parks. The evident intention of all this is to deprive them of sleep. Well and good, the powers have the power to deprive them of sleep, or of anything else for that matter; but why under the sun do they open the gates of the parks at five o'clock in the morning and let the homeless ones go inside and sleep? If it is their intention to deprive them of sleep, why do they let them sleep after five in the morning? And if it is not their intention to deprive them of sleep, why don't they let them sleep earlier in the night?

In this connection, I will say that I came by Green Park that same day, at one in the afternoon, and that I counted scores of the ragged wretches asleep in the grass. It was Sunday afternoon, the sun was fitfully appearing, and the well-dressed West Enders, with their wives and progeny, were out by thousands, taking the air. It was not a pleasant sight for them, those horrible, unkempt, sleeping vagabonds; while the vagabonds themselves, I know, would rather have done their sleeping the night before.

And so, dear soft people, should you ever visit London Town, and see these men asleep on the benches and in the grass, please do not think they are lazy creatures, preferring sleep to work. Know that the powers that be have kept them walking all the night long, and that in the day they have nowhere else to sleep.

Jack London, 1903

After we returned to London, in September, I used to stroll much among the recumbent figures of the unemployed on the grass of Green Park, where, lulled by the ocean roar of the omnibuses on Piccadilly, they drowsed away the hours of the autumnal day. These fellow-men looked more interesting than they probably were, either asleep or awake, and if I could really have got inside their minds I dare say I should have been no more amused than if I had penetrated the consciousness of as many people of fashion in the height of the season. But what I wish to say is that, whether sleeping or waking, they never, any of them, asked me for a penny, or in any wise intimated a wish to divide my wealth with me. If I offered it myself, it was another thing, and it was not refused to the extent of a shilling by the good fellow whose conversation I bought one afternoon when I found him, sitting up in his turfy bed, and mending his coat with needle and thread. I asked him of the times and their badness, him an artisan out of work, taking his misfortune bravely. He was certainly cheerful, and we had some agreeable moments,

So limp a name suits Green Park, which has never achieved the beauty nor established the distinct character of its great neighbours. Its chief glory was the fine series of mansions that lined its eastern side, but when this photograph was taken, c. 1910, destruction had already begun at the northern end, to make room for the Ritz Hotel.

which I could not prolong, because I did not like waking the others, or such of them as might be sleeping.

I did not object to his cheerfulness, though for misery to be cheerful seemed to be rather trivial, and I was better pleased with the impassioned bearing of a pair who passed me another day as I sat on one of the benches beside the path where the trees were dropping their listless leaves. The pair were a father and mother, if I might judge from their having each a babe in their arms and two or three other babes at their heels. They were not actually in tatters, but anything more intensely threadbare than their thin clothes could not be imagined; they were worse than ragged. They looked neither to the right nor to the left, but stared straight on and pressed straight on rather rapidly, with such desperate tragedy in their looks as moved me to that noble terror which the old-fashioned critics used to inculcate as the best effect of tragedy on the stage. I followed them a little way before I gained courage to speak to the man, who seemed to have been sick, and looked more miserable, if there was a choice, than the woman. Then I asked him, superfluously enough (it might have seemed in a ghastly pleasantry, to him) if he was down on his luck. He owned that he was, and in guarantee of his good faith took the shilling I offered him. If his need had apparently been less dire I might have made it a sovereign; but one must not fly in the face of the Providence, which is probably not ill-advised in choosing certain of us to be reduced to absolute destitution. The man smiled a sick, thin-lipped smile which showed his teeth in a sort of pinched

way, but did not speak more; his wife, gloomily unmoved, passed me without a look, and I rather slunk back to my seat, feeling that I had represented, if I had not embodied, society to her.

William Dean Howells, 1905

A SUBSTITUTE FOR THE SEA

Though Victoria Park has not acquired the prestige of either Hyde or Regent's Park, it is not inferior to either of them in natural beauty or brightness of floral decoration. From end to end it is somewhere about a mile and a quarter long, and it is nearly half a mile wide at its broadest part. Every inch of its large area of 217 acres contributes its quota towards brightening the lives of the teeming thousands who dwell in the densely-populated districts surrounding the park. This splendid playground of the East End is quite as dear to the industrial population who frequent it as the sweeping drives and pleasant walks of the West End parks to their fashionable visitors.

The area of the park is so large that it is possible to provide for nearly every form of out-door amusement and recreation. Foremost among these must be placed swimming and bathing, for which this park affords special facilities. As many as 25,000 bathers have been counted on a summer morning before eight o'clock.

In the summer cricket is amply provided for. There are thirty-two pitches on the match-ground, not to speak of the many games of the youngsters who are allowed to set up their stumps or pile up their jackets on any part of the unappropriated ground. For the followers of lawn-tennis there are some thirty-seven courts, all of them free. In the summer band performances are given, which attract considerable audiences. There are four gymnasia, two of which are specially reserved for children. The children certainly are well looked after, and nothing can be pleasanter than to stroll round from point to point and watch the happy little crowds disporting themselves on swings and see-saws, sailing their boats on the waters of the lake, or digging in the sand-pit, apparently quite as happy as though they were within sight and sound of the sea-waves.

Altogether, Victoria Park forms a splendid playground, and though the cost of maintaining it is considerable, it must be admitted that the money is well spent, seeing that it brings brightness to many lives whose lot is not of the happiest.

Lt.-Col. John Sexby, 1898

A Long Time Dying

The main street of Putney used until lately to display some good specimens of the old brick house with richly carved doorways and fair grounds behind. Here stood a fine old country mansion, Fairfax House, whose existence long hung

'Sunday in Victoria Park', as seen by the Illustrated London News *in 1892.*

The animated scene at Mortlake for the finish of the 1895 universities' boat race. The hot favourites Oxford won by the unexpectedly narrow margin of two-and-a-quarter lengths.

in the balance, aesthetic persons pleading passionately for its preservation. The 'jerry builder', however, had his way, and has long since covered the grounds with 'neat' brick tenements and shops. Three or four good old specimens still remain, together with a picturesque roadside inn or 'public' of great antiquity. Indeed throughout the year the place is drowsy enough, but at one season, during the boat-race, it wakes up. All the inns and boathouses are fairly alive with the candidates and their friends and backers, and the river presents an extraordinary scene of animation. Then we hear of nothing but the 'tow-path' and 'slowing off the Soap Works' and of the 'coaching from the bank'. The interest, however, of a contest between a number of mere college lads is fast dying out. In a few years it is likely that these so-called 'Isthmian games' will have been given up.

Percy Fitzgerald, 1893

THE TWO CODES

Football in London rouses itself from its summer's sleep less readily than it does in the provinces, where they keep a vigil on the last night of August that they may the earlier kick the ball when September dawns. In London we are not so precipitous,

and we recognise the right of King Cricket to prolong his life for a few more days if he may. Nevertheless, when the autumn comes football is in the air, and the great professional clubs lose no time in the commencement of their business. Even in August, when the sun is hot o'erhead, and when, according to football law, no matches shall be played under pain of the most grievous penalties – yes, even in this warm, mellow month, if you come with me down to Woolwich or to Tottenham I could show you crowds some thousands strong. And these would be criticising, praising and condemning, hoping and despairing, but all of them yelling, as they watch the first practice games of the season in which old and new players are weighed in the balance and accepted for rejected for the League team as the case may be. This is a time for nervous excitement for all concerned, and indeed in this respect there is only one other period which may be properly likened unto this one upon the threshold of the season's campaign. And that other one is eight months in advance, in the last days of March and the beginning of April, when the proven stalwarts of the season close together for the final bout in which the honours at last are the laurels of absolute and undisputed championship.

It seems to me that few modern pastimes can so conjure up in one's mind a vision of the games of old as this practice football, when the qualities of the players are being tested, and when every mind is on the strain as to how the best

Blackburn Rovers on the attack during their 3–1 FA Cup Final win over Nottinghamshire County at Kennington Oval on 21 March 1891.
The referee was assisted by two umpires.

possible team shall be selected. Every individual of the crowd round the rails has an interest in the result. Either he pays his half-guinea for a season ticket or his admission money every Saturday, and if the team is not to his liking he will want to know the reason why. Nominally the committee is the arbiter and it actually makes the choice of men; but no committee of a professional club in the metropolitan area or anywhere else would dare to neglect the force of public opinion to any substantial extent. You see, it takes some thousands a year to run these professional clubs, and those thousands have to come from the men who are shouting round the green.

And so it happens that when Sandy McTavish, the new forward, who has come all the way from Motherwell, Dumbarton, or the Vale of Leven for four pounds a week, strips himself and bounds into the ring for practice and for judgment, his feelings on analysis are found to be much the same as those of the gladiator in the glorious days of Rome. Sandy skims down the wing like a bird in flight, such are his ease and grace and skill; and at the right moment – thud! and the ball has whizzed into the net, a splendid and most excellent goal. Sandy thus has made his mute appeal. The crowd is appreciative, it screams its pleasure, the latest Scot is the greatest hero, and – it is thumbs up for Sandy. But what if he fumbled and fell, and, perhaps through sheer nervousness,

did nought that was good upon a football field? None would know so well as Sandy that his fate was sealed, and that no mercy awaited him. There are scowls and murmurs of discontent from beyond the touch-line, and, most cutting of all, they are derisive cheers. Poor miserable Sandy knows full well that thumbs are down, and a vision of the second team, with a subsequent ignominious transfer to some other club, comes up in his tortured mind. Yes, for the human view of it, for the strenuousness, the excitement, the doubt, and the stirring episodes of London football, give me the practice games in the early days when the law forbids a real foe.

The other notable and enduring feature of London football is its Rugby section. It has a story all of its own, and the Rugby enthusiast never could see anything in the 'socker' game. It is admitted that 'rugger' is a cult, a superior cult, and though it has its followers by thousands in London, it is not the game of the people as is that played under the rival code of laws. Yet London has always held a glorious place in the Rugby football world, and the public schools and the 'Varsities supply such a constant infusion of good new blood, so that when the fame of Richmond and Blackheath fade away, we shall be listening for the crack of Rugby doom.

Henry Leach, 1901

Chapter 5

STREETS AND BUILDINGS

One hundred years ago the streets of London were noisy and dirty. That is not to say that nothing has changed, for the quality of the noise and dirt were unlike our own. For us a horse in the street is a rare and usually a solitary sight. Its sound is a charming clip-clop. In the 1890s the noise of a hundred horses advancing along Cheapside or the Strand was like a cavalry charge, and a cavalry charge over echoing wooden blocks rather than the mud of Flanders. To this was added the rumbling and creaking of the carts and drays that choked the streets of this great trading city, and the crack of the carters' whips. The human contribution came from the newsboys with their shouts of ' 'orrible murder!' or 'winners!', and from the costermongers and pavement hawkers crying their wares. In the side streets comparative immunity from traffic noise often came at the price of exposure to the street musician, either the solo performer on the barrel organ or the dreaded troupes of the petticoat quartet or the German band, whose performances amounted to little more than aural blackmail.

The filthiness of the streets was the common fate of all cities where the horse was the mainstay of the transport system, and London, as the largest, had the greatest problem. Despite the efforts of the orderly boys, the road sweepers and the dustmen, the presence of thousands of horses and their stables in the heart of the town polluted the air quite as much as today's petrol fumes. Road accidents were if anything more frequent than with us, though less often fatal. Horses were always slipping or bolting, and one of the characteristic sights of London was an interested crowd watching the efforts of drivers and policemen to raise one that had fallen.

A very great change in the appearance of the streets was produced in the 1890s by the introduction of illuminated advertising. Returning home in 1899 after a long residence in France Charles Whibley found that 'the unaccustomed eye is conscious of a new glitter, and divines not whence it comes. At night the problem is easily solved. The hideous sky-signs, which applaud in changing colours the merits of some intolerable drug, or implore you to buy some sustaining compound for your stomach's sake, might transform the face of a prairie.'

There can be few people who remember St Martin's Place without Edith Cavell, and none, surely, who saw General Gordon in occupation of her island. He was only a passing show. The original of Edward Onslow Ford's memorial was erected at Chatham in 1890. This copy was exhibited outside the National Portrait Gallery in 1902, before being shipped to Khartoum.

IRRECONCILABLE VIEWS

The railway bridge that crosses Ludgate Hill was once the occasion of a fierce controversy. It was a struggle between the artistic and the practical – between the aesthetic and the economic. It was the old controversy – not quite so old as the hills, but certainly as old as the very first time when industrial science of the rudest form began to turn the hills to account for the supposed benefit of man. Why, then, should not Ludgate Hill come on for her turn in the discussion? Ludgate Hill 'waited for her time – which time came,' as Carlyle says, discoursing on a quite different subject. The time came when it was proposed to span Ludgate Hill with this railway bridge. The railway bridge itself is by no means an unlovely object. Regarded as a railway bridge merely, it is rather a fine work of art. Its iron tracery is delicate and picturesque. But then, as a bridge crossing Ludgate Hill and cutting off from Fleet Street the view of St. Paul's – how about it when considered in that way? Thus the controversy arose. Mr. Ruskin struck in with characteristic gallantry, and condemned the practical principle which would spoil so fine a street view for the convenience of a railway and its passengers. I remember favouring the public with some opinions of my own on the same subject in a newspaper with which I was then connected, and which newspaper I have long outlived. My opinions merely said ditto to Mr. Ruskin. Yes, it was a

fine street view – one of the finest street views in London – which met the eyes of those who looked up from Fleet Street to Ludgate Hill and St. Paul's. It was a grand historic sight. Many of the old houses were still standing, and the whole scene retained much of its mediaeval aspect. Let it be frankly owned that the view is spoiled now – utterly spoiled. The railway bridge bounds the horizon of one walking from Fleet Street. He sees nothing but that; thinks of nothing but that. Perhaps I should rather put it this way – he hardly sees the bridge, for he does not think about it; but he sees nothing, also, and thinks of nothing. Now, in the old days, a goodly proportion of the wayfarers could hardly fail to be struck by the hill, and the Cathedral on its brow. But then the men of practical progress, even if they are willing to admit all this, will ask us what are the artistic or aesthetic glimpses of a few visionaries and dreamers when compared with the comfort and convenience of the thousands and thousands who pass along in the railway, backwards and forwards, every day?

There it is, you see. If the controversy were to go on all over again, I should not take part in it. Not that I have changed my opinions in the least as to the general principle or as to this particular instance. But where is the good of arguing on such a subject? The artistic always goes down before what is called the practical in a matter like that.

Justin MacCarthy, 1893

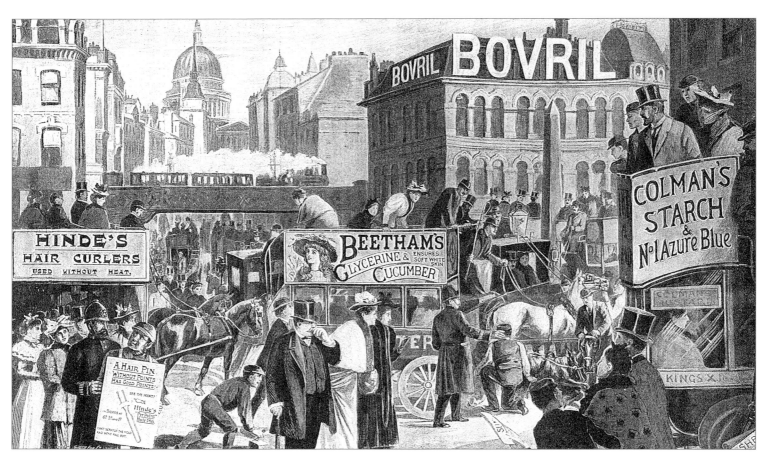

This co-operative 1896 advertisement shows, among many other things, including an orderly boy and a fallen omnibus horse, the much-contested Ludgate Hill railway bridge, itself now becoming a quaint memory.

There are infinite attractions in London. I have seen many foreign cities, but I know none so commodious, or, let me add, so beautiful. I know of nothing in any foreign city equal to the view down Fleet Street, walking along the north side from the corner of Fetter Lane. It is often said that this has been spoiled by the London, Chatham, and Dover Railway bridge over Ludgate Hill; I think, however, the effect is more imposing now than it was before the bridge was built. Time has already softened it; it does not obtrude itself; it adds greatly to the sense of size, and makes us doubly aware of the movement of life, the colossal circulation to which London owes so much of its impressiveness. We gain more by this than we lose by the infraction of some pedant's canon about the artistically correct intersection of right lines. Vast as is the world below the bridge, there is a vaster still on high, and when trains are passing, the steam from the engine will throw the dome of St. Paul's into the clouds, and make it seem as though there were a commingling of earth and some far-off mysterious palace in dreamland. I am not very fond of Milton, but I admit that he does at times put me in mind of Fleet Street.

Samuel Butler, 1882

A FORETASTE OF NEW YORK

What a turmoil there is about Ludgate Circus! What roofs, what telegraph wires – what placards, ensigns, advertisements high in air – what omnibuses, carriages, carts, cabs, donkey-carts, the cart which the costermonger pushes before him,

the mail-carts, the carts of the *Star* newspaper, equally red with those of Her Majesty's mail, the oblong carts of the Parcel Post – all these are on the earth, and make the firm ground look like a quaking bog. The great signs that are hung out across the fronts of houses, and on the tops of houses, make Ludgate Circus look like a part of New York. The Obelisk rises out of the throng in the street like a solitary camel's head out of the crowd of a pilgrimage. The spire rising out of the pell-mell has more significance. It invites us all to look up – up – above 'the city's rout and noise and humming.' I wonder how many wayfarers in each day are touched by the appeal of the spire and look upwards! I wonder how many who do look upwards are impelled thereto by the spire's silent admonition, and are the better for it!

Justin MacCarthy, 1893

THAT FUNNY DRAGON

The changes which London has undergone in the past twenty or thirty years are so great that I can quite imagine a visitor formerly familiar with the old streets unable now to find his way from Temple Bar to the Tower. The very first thing to meet his eyes would be the huge mass of the Law Courts, where formerly was a rookery of dilapidated, if picturesque, houses. Then where is Temple Bar? Where is the dingy front of Child's Bank with its curious little room over the arch? Where, on the opposite side, are the familiar oyster shop and the old Cock? All are gone, and we might be better

This photograph of Ludgate Circus in the late 1880s gives a good impression of the speed of the carts and carriages, and the bustle of the pedestrians. It also shows that the London mist did more than any bridge to obscure the view of St Paul's.

Designing the Temple Bar griffin monument was one of the many official chores of Sir Horace Jones, architect to the City of London. It was erected in 1880, a decade after Temple Bar itself was removed.

resigned to their loss if we could persuade ourselves that the region still vaguely denominated Temple Bar had been improved in the process of alteration.

I have not heard any adequate reason advanced for the removal of the old archway. Some people said it obstructed the highway; to which the obvious answer was, 'Make the street wider and leave Temple Bar in the middle.' That is what they have done in Paris. If the road was obstructed, why was that funny Dragon set up?

I regret its removal, because it was extremely beautiful in itself, and because it had many interesting associations. There has been a kind of crusade against Wren's works of late years; and Temple Bar was doomed from the first. The age that spared not the College of Physicians was not likely to respect Temple Bar, even if it had been what it was not, a city gate.

W. J. Loftie, 1891

CLASSICAL CALM

I should omit one of the most remarkable features in London's street life if I did not point to the almost classical perfection of the police. The London policeman is usually tall and of fine appearance. In his dark blue uniform he does not possess the military swagger of his Berlin *confrère*, nor is his weapon a sword, but only a truncheon kept in a leather casing. He is

courteous and modest to everybody, and really a marvel for the classical calmness with which he directs the enormous street traffic. He simply raises his hand and the long row of carriages comes to a stand, like the flood in the Red Sea at the passage of the Jews. Now the traffic from the cross streets passes in front of us. Two or three minutes more and our street is open again, and the vehicles from the cross street have to wait in their turn. This continues ceaselessly from morning until evening like automatic clockwork, without noise or excitement of any kind. Assisted in his work is the London policeman by the Englishman's characteristic sense of law and order. A movement of the hand is sufficient for him, where the Berlin cabdriver requires loud and threatening words. And the London policeman is chivalrous, too, with ladies and children. Touching, indeed, is it to observe the considerateness with which he conducts some old beggar woman or little children through the crowd from one side of the street to the other.

Carl Peters, 1904

THE STRAND MADELEINE

It is hard for a somewhat dreamy personage like myself to take the Strand quite seriously. One has made it so unreal – one has hashed up in such inextricable confusion the real and the unreal. The scent that comes from Rimmel's shop brings back all youth to me. Why? Simply because I used to look into Rimmel's windows and inhale their scents when I was a very young man. Nothing carries with it a richer association than the breath of some scent. It is like magic. Music itself – which *is* magic – can hardly equal it. You are wandering along the streets thinking of nothing – along the Strand – and you are utterly commonplace. And suddenly some breath of perfume is borne in upon you – from a flower-girl's roses, or even from the made-up contents of Rimmel's window-cases – and behold! one is living all at once in another and an enchanted world – the world one lived in or fancied he was living in years and years ago. Once, not long since, I was passing down the Strand, and there were some repairs going on – and I caught the odour of a pitch-kettle – and in a moment I was back to the seaport home of my boyhood again, and to the sound of the breaking waves.

Justin MacCarthy, 1893

BROADWAY AND THE STRAND

One reason, I think, why London is so much more striking is in the unbroken line which the irregularly divided streets often present to the passer. Here is a chance for architecture to extend, while with us it has only a chance to tower, on the short up-town block which is the extreme dimension of our proudest edifice, public or private. Another reason is in the London atmosphere, which deepens and heightens all the effects, while the lunar bareness of our perspectives mercilessly reveals the facts. After you leave the last cliff behind on lower Broadway the only incident of the long,

Joseph Pennell's sketch of the
Strand, made in 1889, shows
the part that was soon to be so
greatly changed by the Aldwych
development, for which all the
buildings on the left were swept
away. Notice the orderly boy (see
page 84) at his dangerous work
in the path of the oncoming
buses.

straight avenue which distracts you from the varied commonplace of the commercial structures on either hand is the loveliness of Grace Church; but in the Strand and Fleet Street you have a succession of edifices which overwhelm you with the sense of a life in which trade is only one of the incidents. If the day is such as a lover of the picturesque would choose, or may rather often have without choosing, when the scene is rolled in vaporous smoke, and a lurid gloom hovers from the hidden sky, you have an effect of majesty and grandeur that no other city can offer. As the shadow momently thickens or thins in the absence or the presence of the yellowish-green light, the massive structures are shown or hid, and the meaner houses render the rifts between more impressively chasmal. The tremendous volume of life that flows through the narrow and winding channels past the dim cliffs and pinnacles, and the lower banks which the lesser buildings form, is such that the highest tide of Broadway or Fifth Avenue seems a scanty ebb beside it. The swelling and towering omnibuses, the huge trucks and wagons and carriages, the impetuous hansoms and the more sobered four-wheelers, the pony-carts, donkey-carts, handcarts, and bicycles which fearlessly find their way amid the turmoil, with foot-passengers winding in and out, and covering the sidewalks with their multitude, give the effect of a single monstrous organism, which writhes swiftly along the channel where it had run in the figure of a flood till you were tired of that metaphor. You are now a molecule of that vast organism, as you sit under your umbrella on your omnibus-

The Strand and Fleet Street seen from the east end of St Clement Danes in the early 1890s, with the new Law Courts – already a little soiled – on the left. Note the gentleman in the white topper composedly reading his evening paper amid all this bustle.

top, with the public waterproof apron across your knees, and feel in supreme degree the insensate exultation of being part of the largest thing of its kind in the world, or perhaps the universe.

William Dean Howells, 1905

STARTLING NEWS

For inventive energy I think our newspaper-selling boys and men might hold their own against most of their brothers in the trade. The New York newsboy is an astounding little fellow, with his indomitable energy, and his unwearying good spirits, and his quenchless eagerness for trade; but I do not think he allows himself to invent much. I remember being stopped once in a cab, as I was driving home from a theatre on the Strand, by a boy selling newspapers, who implored me to buy the latest edition, containing the full account of the shooting of Mr. Parnell that evening by Mr. Charles Bradlaugh. I did not purchase, and the event was not recorded in the morning journals of the following day.

Justin MacCarthy, 1893

The evening papers, or at all events the smaller ones, seem almost to live on racing news. From one o'clock in the afternoon till late at night the streets of London resound with the cry of 'Winner! All the winners!' and the monotony of the announcement becomes such a nuisance that the occasional "'Orrible Murder at 'Ampstead!" or "Shocking Outrage at Regent's Park!" affords quite a pleasant relief to the ear.

Montagu Williams, 1892

THE FLOWER GIRLS' REFUGE

Piccadilly Circus is a brilliant whirl! Vehicles of every size roll hither and thither. Pedestrians, obviously much concerned for the safety of their bones, step briskly from the circumference to the centre, or *vice versa*, sometimes sacrificing dignity to a comical little trot. The air quivers with a thousand blended sounds, in which nothing is clear but the frequent tinkle of the 'bus conductor's bell. In the centre of the changeful scene, the bevy of flower girls, seated on the steps of the Shaftesbury Fountain, are models of industrious and stolid indifference.

They are fashioning buttonholes. In a small way they are rivals of the great florists in Regent Street or Piccadilly. How artistically their stock is disposed! Delicate roses are perched coquettishly on stakes a foot high, which stand in baskets of dark-green moss. And what colour combinations! Every vagary of taste is anticipated. Business is brisk. Between attending to customers and preparing for them they seem to have scarcely an idle minute. But as the sun goes down you may sometimes see a flower girl absorbed in her evening paper, while gilded London throbs around her.

P. F. William Ryan, 1903

A BUNGLED ATTEMPT

It is doubtless a signal proof of being a London-lover *quand même* that one should undertake an apology for so bungled an attempt at a great public place as Hyde Park Corner. It is certain that the improvements and embellishments recently enacted there have only served to call further attention to the poverty of the elements, and to the fact that this poverty is terribly illustrative of general conditions. The place is the beating heart of the great West End, yet its main features are a shabby, stuccoed hospital, the low park-gates in their neat but unimposing frame, the drawing-room windows of Apsley House, and of the commonplace frontages on the little terrace beside it; to which must be added, of course, the only item in the whole prospect that is in the least

"'ORRIBLE AND RE-VOLTIN' DETAILS, SIR!"

The enterprising London newsboy as portrayed by the inimitable Phil May.

Piccadilly Circus was still looking unimaginably elegant when this photograph was taken c. 1900, although the Shaftesbury Memorial (Eros) of 1893 hardly matched Nash's architecture. But destruction had already begun in the Circus with the intrusion of Shaftesbury Avenue in the 1880s, and soon the owners of its banal new shops would discover the profitable delights of advertising.

Hyde Park Corner is now just a traffic jam from which we all hope to escape as quickly as possible. This 1894 sketch suggests something of the charm that made Henry James happy to dawdle in his hansom.

In 1905 this was the view eastwards from the junction of Knightsbridge and Brompton Road, over the statue of Field Marshal Lord Strathnairn. Albert Gate Terrace is on the left. The 'monstrous pile' was still luxury flats. It did not become the Hyde Park Hotel until 1908.

monumental – the arch spanning the private road beside the gardens of Buckingham Palace. This structure is now bereaved of the rueful effigy which used to surmount it – the Iron Duke in the guise of a tin soldier – and has not been enriched by the transaction as much as might have been expected. There is a fine view of Piccadilly and Knightsbridge, and of the noble mansions, as the house-agents call them, of Grosvenor Place, together with a sense of generous space beyond the vulgar little railing of the Green Park; but, except for the impression that there would be room for something better, there is nothing in all this that speaks to the imagination: almost as much as the grimy desert of Trafalgar Square the prospect conveys the idea of an opportunity wasted.

None the less has it on a fine day in spring an expressiveness of which I shall not pretend to explain the source further than by saying that the flood of life and luxury is immeasurably great there. The edifices are mean, but the social stream itself is monumental, and to an observer not purely stolid there is more excitement and suggestion than I can give a reason for in the long, distributed waves of traffic, with the steady policemen marking their rhythm, which roll together and apart for so many hours. Then the great dim city becomes bright and kind, the pall of smoke turns into a veil of haze carelessly worn, the air is coloured and almost scented by the presence of the biggest society in the world, and most of the things that meet the eye – or perhaps I should say more of them, for the most in London is, no doubt, ever the realm of the dingy – present themselves as 'well-appointed'. Everything shines more or less, from the window-panes to the dog-collars. So it all looks, with its myriad variations and qualifications, to one who surveys it over the apron of a hansom, while that vehicle of vantage, better than any box at the opera, spurts and slackens with the current.

Henry James, 1888

A MONSTROUS PILE

So recently as Lady Morgan's day, Knightsbridge and Albert Gate were almost as rustic and countryfied as parts of Hammersmith Road. The little Albert Gate Terrace is a survival of these times. Each has its garden in front, evidence of its suburban character; and a tiny one behind, with a view of the undulating park and its trees beyond. These quaint, interesting houses, which suggest Church Row at Clapham, have but short tenure of existence. The monstrous pile beside them, 'The Mansions', gives significant warning that their place is wanted. Further on we come to the handsome Knightsbridge Barracks, a goodly specimen of architecture on the Park side, monumental, and a decided improvement to the neighbourhood. Beside it stood until recently a huge riding school, which has been levelled, perhaps to give place to the irrepressible 'flats'.

Percy Fitzgerald, 1893

Chapter 6

SHOPPING

As an international shopping centre London had lagged well behind Paris during most of the nineteenth century, though it naturally led the way in England. Cheapside and St Paul's Churchyard maintained a reputation for solid worth. Bond Street, Piccadilly, and St James's Street could compare with the best, and Regent Street was used abroad as a standard symbol for London, rather as Big Ben or Tower Bridge are today. But Oxford Street was still partly residential, and its shops were small and insignificant. Nobody thought of going to Chelsea or Knightsbridge to shop, and the Brompton Road was no more fashionable than the Walworth Road.

It was the development of great department stores that transformed the situation. They usually started as draperies, though just occasionally ironmongery or grocery provided the foundation. Beginning with a single shop the enterprising owners would gradually absorb their neighbours, and once they had acquired a sufficiently large terrace, would begin to think about rebuilding on a monumental scale. The key to this would be the possibility of gaining control of a whole block, including the properties in the side turnings and behind the existing shops. In 1900 this was scarcely possible in Bond Street or Piccadilly, but practical in less central and traditional areas. Once size had become as important as location, the attention of shoppers was readily directed to the western end of Oxford Street, and to Westbourne Grove, Knightsbridge, and the Brompton Road. Several of our great modern department stores were built in their present form at this time, Harrod's, for example, in 1901–5, and Selfridge's from 1909.

In sharp contrast to the changing patterns of middle-class shopping the marketing of the poor continued along its age-old lines. Those with small and precarious incomes were forced to buy in tiny quantities from corner shops where the farthing and the ounce were the standard units of trade. The main shopping of the week was conducted in one of the many street markets, either on Saturday night, when a carnival atmosphere prevailed, or even more cheaply (and illegally) on Sunday morning, when the costermongers tried to dispose of their remaining stock.

One of the largest street markets of south London occupied Lower Marsh, New Cut, and Great Charlotte Street (the last two now combined as The Cut), on either side of Waterloo Road. This is Great Charlotte Street in the 1880s. The extraordinary building in the background was the Ring, formerly the Surrey Chapel, in Blackfriars Road.

Few parts of London have changed so much since the war, or so much for the worse, as St Paul's Churchyard. This view from the top of Ludgate Hill shows the ladies' shopping paradise c. 1908. Apart from the cathedral, the only survivor of the Blitz was the Chapter House (the dark building right of centre) which has been restored minus the attic storey.

THE LADIES' PARADISE

No picture of the City of London, no matter how hurried and incomplete it is, may neglect St. Paul's Churchyard. Here, in close proximity to the Cathedral railings, is a row of handsome shops, beloved of the fair sex. Along the greater part of the roadway no wheeled traffic is allowed – a fact which secures its patrons from the splash of mud in bad weather. Here, for the first time in the City, we find a crowd of ladies. It is the only place where there is a collection of shops for their benefit, and the shops are of an excellence which has earned for 'St. Paul's Churchyard' fame throughout Britain. As a contrast to the congregations of men we have been among, St. Paul's Churchyard is singularly striking. Men there are, of course, but the bulk of the people are ladies, crowding round the shop windows. Into the roadway do they extend, and only near the railings is progress easy. Any attempt at rapid walking in busy City streets only leads to exasperation; and in Cheapside and St. Paul's Churchyard only the slowest progress is possible.

Charles Turner, 1903

Two elegant window-shoppers admire the latest fashions for 1892 in St Paul's Churchyard.

My Queen Vel-Vel

Is the Daintiest DRESS FABRIC the modern loom has given to the fashionable world. For softness and delicacy of surface, "MY QUEEN" VEL-VEL equals the best Lyons Silk Velvet, for which it forms an attractive substitute. The depths and richness of Blacks in "MY QUEEN" VEL-VEL have never been equalled, while the New Shade Card contains nearly 200 colours, including every conceivable Art Shade.

The view north up Old Bond Street, seen from the corner of Stafford Street, c. 1910. The shop on the right, the largest in this area of huge rents, was occupied by Russell and Allen, court dressmakers, furriers and milliners.

A CONFIDENCE TRICK

Of all the streets you have ever read of, Bond Street is the most disappointing. (But it is also the most surprising when you go to buy things in it.) 'Stepping into her carriage in Bond Street,' says the society novelist, 'the Duchess gave an order in a low voice to her coachman.' When you come to see the actual Duchess in that narrow alley-way, it seems somehow as though her grandeur had lost itself in a slum. It is a narrow, tortuous, congested lane, which, for some queer reason, has got itself established as the most expensive thoroughfare in the world. It is mean looking, but it is priceless. The very unimpressive shops which line its scanty side-walks are each leased at a figure representing a higher rate of income than many important personages in the professions, or in commercial life, enjoy. And their contents are priced at figures in conformity with their rents.

It is not, one believes, that you can obtain anything of a much better quality in Bond Street than in other parts of London. It is simply the power of the tradition, encountered everywhere in England, that makes its wares expensive. It would almost seem as if those who occupy the street had long ago said amongst themselves, 'Here we are – right in the middle of the people who have got the money. We'll make them pay, – because they've got it, – we'll make them pay exceedingly. Why shouldn't we, if we can?' And they have done so, and it is another of the indications of the great wealth which is of London and of England that they should continue to succeed in doing so.

J. H. M. Abbott, 1905

THE ETERNAL SHOPPER

I am confident that if a million of women of all classes could by any possibility be placed in a Palace of Truth, and interrogated straitly as to what they liked best in all London, the vast majority of them would answer, 'The Shops.' Indeed, you may easily, and without any undue inquisitiveness, find this out for yourself by simply taking (in May for choice) a morning or afternoon walk down Oxford Street or Regent Street. Every shop of note will have its quota of would-be buyers, trembling on the brink of irrevocable purchase; its treble, nay, quadruple row of admiring females, who appear to find this by far the most attractive mode of getting through the day. I would go further, and say that as regards the more persevering among them, it is difficult to imagine that they ever have any other occupation at all.

The shops of London have wonderfully improved in quite recent years; not perhaps, so much in actual quality, as in arrangement and taste. Labels with 'dropsical figures' of shillings and perfectly invisible pence have, as in Dickens's time, still their charm for us; but other things have changed. Everything could, to those who 'knew,' always be bought best in London; but

'An Afternoon Walk in Regent Street' records the ageless delights of shopping, as enjoyed in 1891.

I was, so with the blood all a-streamin' down my face, I rose my 'at graceful an' says, 'I beg your parding.' That's all I says, 'I beg your parding.' I crushed 'im *with breedin'!*

Harry Furniss, 1919

THE UNIVERSAL PROVIDER

It is impossible to mark off certain districts on a map of London and assign to each a particular class of customers. Of course, those who want the best of everything without regard to cost generally find what they require without leaving the aristocratic quarter of which Bond Street and Regent Street are well-known arteries. But no lady who finds in shopping one of the pleasures of her life fails to make regular pilgrimages to Westbourne Grove. The neighbourhood has an atmosphere of its own. Here shopping assumes the dignity of a cult. The pavements are generally crowded with smartly dressed women chatting earnestly – it is all of prices, bargains, catalogues, and such things. In Westbourne Grove man realises his insignificance. That is probably the reason why his absence is so conspicuous.

P. F. William Ryan, 1903

Bishop's Road is continued to the Kensington border of the borough by Westbourne Grove, famous as one of the great shopping centres of London, for here is the great establishment founded by Mr. William Whiteley, the 'Universal Provider', who was shot dead in the lace department of the establishment in 1907. His murderer was saved from the gallows by a gust of public feeling which the Home Secretary deemed it imprudent to disregard.

W. W. Hutchings, 1909

everything was not always displayed to the best advantage. To dress a shop-front well was in old days hardly considered a British trait. But 'nous avons changé tout cela.' Now, even the Paris boulevard, that Paradise of good Americans, has, except perhaps in the matter of trees and wide streets, little to teach us. 'The wealth of Ormus and of Ind' that the shops of Regent Street and Bond Street display, their gold embroideries and wonderfully woven silks, tending to make a kleptomaniac out of the very elect, – these it would be hard indeed to beat. Not Solomon in all his glory was arrayed like one of these.

Mrs E. T. Cook, 1902

BREEDING

George Grossmith had many good stories to tell; one that always amused me was his story, which he related as a true one, of a costermonger who thought he would enjoy his holiday taking a walk through the West End. 'Yes, Mr. Grossmith, I dress myself up spiff, and goes up Regency Street. I was a-lookin' at some photergraafs in a shop winder when a swell bloke wid a lydy on his arm gives me a shove and sends my 'ead clean through that 'ere winder. Did I cuss and swear? Did I use bad langvidge? No. I remembered w'ere

A GREAT STORE

'The stores' is a common phrase in the trivial common talk of everyday life. It is generally understood that at one of those comprehensive emporiums practically everything may be ordered. This is true to a certain extent only, for it must be remembered that there are 'stores' which cater for the humblest strata of the middle class. Those are naturally less ambitious in their aims than the establishments which supply the needs of the rich and comparatively rich. Without quitting the premises of one of these latter, with their acres of warerooms, their tireless 'lifts', their well-drilled assistants, it is almost impossible to ask for anything which will not be promptly yours. Do you want a house built? You have but to give the necessary instructions. Would you like to decide upon your furniture? In a moment you will find yourself inspecting improvised drawing-rooms and dining-rooms, bedrooms and billiard-rooms, studies and kitchens.

Do you want your greenhouse equipped? From where you stand possibly you can see a tangle of shrubs and plants, and

Under the leadership of William Whiteley, the notorious 'universal provider', Westbourne Grove became one of the great shopping streets of the period, where the department stores 'advertise themselves, modestly, to provide everything, from a coffin to a hired guest'.

nestling amidst them the flowers of the season in full bloom. Do you love animals? Then visit the zoological department, and buy a monkey or a puppy, a kitten or a canary. A lion or a tiger may not be included in the stock on hand, but if your ambition lies in that direction your order will be booked and the stores van will soon deposit the exile from African veldt or Indian jungle at your doorstep. Your wife can purchase her daughter's trousseau in one room, while in another you obtain the impedimenta incidental to a shooting expedition. Pass through the 'lamp and glass' department. It reminds one somehow of a scene in a pantomime, for there are numerous lights though it is noonday, and the flood of colour is rich

The American tycoon Gordon Selfridge opened his great department store in Oxford Street in 1909. It is seen here shortly afterwards. Selfridge employed several architects on the huge building, which was not completed until 1928.

and dazzling. Next door are washing tubs and washing boards, pails, mangles, and ladders. Pots and pans are not far away. Move on, and you tread on a gorgeous carpet: all around are carpets stacked in huge rolls. One resembling a great green avenue is unfolded that a lady may judge of its effect. Turn in this direction, and you see silks glistening in glorious little multi-coloured billows, where they are strewn over a long counter for the satisfaction of likely purchasers. A few steps further, and the confectionary department is in sight. Here there are many ladies having lunch. Some are indulging in the trifles on which woman alone can live and thrive – and shop! Others are enjoying fare of the more substantial sort. Full recital of the resources of the 'stores' is impossible. When you have bought your medicines, your literature, your pictures, your saddlery, the latest bicycle and electric plant, flowers for the epergnes, bacon, eggs, and vegetables, fish, poultry, boots, and butter, you may, if you have time, step aside and sit for your photograph, having first made a special toilet, beginning with the bath and ending with the hairdresser and manicurist. Even then the 'stores' have not been fully explored!

P. F. William Ryan, 1903

CIRCULATING MORALS

Ladies would appear but seldom to buy books; they always hire. A morning spent at Smith's or Mudie's is curiously instructive as to the methods pursued by them in the search for light literature. The library counters then usually exhibit a double or treble row of women, with a very faint sprinkling of elderly men, all waiting, in varying degrees of patience, for their turn. Several of the ladies have considerately brought pet dogs, which they hold by the chain, the dear little animals being meanwhile thoughtfully engaged in entangling themselves round all the other customers' legs.

'Have you some nice, new, *good* novels?' asks a plaintive materfamilias, with a stolid-faced bevy of half-grown up daughters behind her, just out of the schoolroom. 'Something, you know, that is quite fit for young girls; no problems, or pasts, or anything of that kind.'

The young man looks nonplussed. 'We have Miss Yonge's latest,' he suggests; 'or Maeterlinck's *Life of the Bee*, just out –'

'Oh! Maeterlinck is so very Maeterlincky, you know. And do you think that he's always quite *safe*?'

'I assure you, madam, you will find him so in this instance,' urges the young man.

'Well, bees are, of course, interesting; and very nice and proper too, I'm sure; but I myself prefer the lives of celebrated people. Mr. Gladstone's Life, for instance? Oh, it's not *written* yet, is it? What a bore! Well, I suppose it's no use our waiting. . . . And Miss Yonge, no, thank you. . . . You see, she died last year, and then she's so very Early-Victorian!'

The man, seeing that it is to be a long business, gives up the problem for the moment, and moves in despair to the next customer.

Now it is the turn of a little old lady, with a deprecating

Mudie's great circulating library, which exercised a powerful unofficial censorship over Victorian literature, was already losing its unique position under the double blow of free public libraries and cheap publishing when this sketch was made in 1901. It probably shows the New Oxford Street branch.

manner: 'I want something nice, and not too clever,' she murmured: 'something I can *knit* over, you know, after breakfast. No, *not* religious, I somehow find that's too depressing. How would this do?' as she picked up a volume that was flaunting itself on the counter, '*Sir Richard Calmady*. I think I'd like that, – if it's at all like *Sir George Tressady*.'

'No, madam, not at all the sort of thing for you,' the young man hastened to say with an air of authority. 'Allow *me*. Try *this*; this is a very safe book, Miss Edna Lyall's latest, *In Spite of All*. This (confidentially) is an author we always recommend.'

Now there bustled up a young-old lady with fuzzy hair and a sailor hat: 'I want all the most go-ahead novels you have,' she cried: 'somethin' really startling, somethin' that'll keep you awake and excited all through.'

This lady being fortunately in a hurry, was quickly got rid of with a judicious mixture of Hall Caine, Guy Boothby, and Marie Corelli, in equal quantities.

Finally there came a nondescript, pudding-faced young woman, who said, vaguely, as if fulfilling a painful duty: 'I want a novel. What is being read now?' She, however, proved very amenable, and went off dutifully with *Elizabeth's Visits*, *The Love-letters of Anonyma*, and the *Transvaal War*.

What vast knowledge of human nature must, one thinks,

But for the costumes this drawing could almost as well have been made in the Charing Cross Road today as in 1901. Certainly this shop at the corner of Great Newport Street is still involved in the trade. What would the owners give to swap their own stock for that of 1901?

these young men at the libraries possess! They seem to enact the part of general literary adviser to the enormous feminine public. They know their types well, too: they rarely mistake. They may almost be said to form the minds of their customers; and they may, they possibly do, rule over a large proportion of human opinion.

Mrs. E. T. Cook, 1902

THE SPIDER'S WEB

Book-shops are very inadequate in London; so few are they indeed, that one is tempted to wonder what the 'five millions, in the richest city in the world' read? In most foreign towns book-shops are to be found, in twos and threes, in every important street; in English provincial towns, if you want a book, you are usually directed to 'a stationer's'; and even in London, book-shops must diligently be sought

for, though, when found, they are, it must be confessed, usually very good.

Second-hand book-shops are more plentiful than new book-shops; and these are mostly strangely dark, dingy, and rambling places, where the depressed proprietor rarely seems to wish to part with any of his dusty stock-in-trade, but sits apart in dusky recesses, moody and abstracted like Eugene Aram, annotating a catalogue. He is the unique tradesman who does not appear to want to sell his goods. After he has got over his annoyance at being disturbed, – and if you do happen to come to terms with him, – he will, as likely as not, heave a deep sigh as he turns to search for some very second-hand sheets of brown paper to enwrap the second-hand treasure. These old book-shops, with their outlying 'twopenny' and 'fourpenny' boxes, are generally to be found on the busy city thoroughfares, as if by intent to entrap the unwary and impecunious scholar on his way home from his office desk to his little suburban home. In such spiders' webs of temptation he has been known to spend, in one fatal half-hour, all the money destined for the butcher's bill, or for the gas rate!

Mrs. E. T. Cook, 1902

LESS JEWISH THAN HESTER STREET

The emotions are not at one's bidding, and if one calls upon them, they are very apt not to come. I promised myself some very signal ones, of a certain type, from going to the Sunday market of the Jews in what was once Petticoat Lane, but now, with the general cleaning up and clearing out of the slums, has got itself called by some much finer and worthier name. But, really, I had seen much Jewisher things in Hester Street, on our own East Side. The market did not begin so early as I had been led to expect it would. The blazing forenoon of my visit was more than half gone, and yet there was no clothes' auction, which was said to be the great thing to see. But by nine o'clock there seemed to be everything else for sale under that torrid July sun, in the long booths and shelters of the street and sidewalks: meat, fish, fruit, vegetables, glassware, ironware, boots and shoes, china and crockery, women's tawdry finery, children's toys, furniture, pictures, succeeding one another indiscriminately, old and new, and cried off with an incessant jargon of bargaining, pierced with shrill screams of extortion and expostulation. A few mild, slim, young London policemen sauntered, apparently unseeing, unhearing, among the fevered, nervous Semitic crowd, in which the Oriental types were by no means so marked as in New York, though there was a greater number of red Jews than I had noted before. The most monumental features of the scene were the gorgeous scales of wrought brass, standing at intervals along the street, and arranged with seats, like swings, for the weighing of such Hebrews as wished to know their tonnage; apparently they have a passion for knowing it.

William Dean Howells, 1905

PATTER

This morning, being Sunday, went to Petticoat Lane and enjoyed myself.

On turning the corner to go into Middlesex Street, as it is now called, the first thing I saw was a little girl – a Jewess – being tackled for selling Belgian buttonhole flags by two policemen who ultimately marched her off to the police station.

In the Lane, first of all, was a 'Royal Ascot Jockey Scales' made of brass and upholstered in gaudy red velvet – a penny a time. A very fat man was being weighed and looked a little distressed on being given his ticket.

'Another stone,' he told the crowd mournfully.

'You'll have to eat less pork,' some one volunteered and we all laughed.

Next door to the Scales was a man selling gyroscopes. 'Something scientific, amusing as well as instructive, illustrating the principles of gravity and stability. What I show you is what I sell – price one shilling. Who?'

I stopped next at a stall containing nothing but caps – 'any size, any colour, any pattern, a shilling apiece – now then!' This show was being run by two men – a Jew in a fur cap on one side of the stall and a very powerful-looking sort of Captain Cuttle on the other – a seafaring man, almost as broad as he was long, with a game leg and the voice of a skipper in a hurricane. Both these men were selling caps at a prodigious pace, and with the insouciance of tradesmen sure of their custom. The skipper would seize a cap, chuck it across to a timid prospective purchaser, and, if he dropped it, chuck him over another, crying, with a 'yo-heave-ho' boisterousness, 'Oh! what a game, what a bees' nest.'

Upon the small head of another customer he would squash down his largest sized cap saying at once:–

'There, you look the finest gentleman – oh! ah! a little too large.'

At which we all laughed, the customer looked silly, but took no offence.

'Try this,' yells the skipper above the storm, and takes off his own cap. 'Oh! ye needn't be afraid – I washed my hair last – year.' (Laughter.)

Then to his partner, the Jew on the other side of the stall, 'Oh! what a face you've got. Here! 6d. for any one who can tell me what it is. Why not take it to the trenches and get it smashed in?'

The Jew wore spectacles and had a soft ingratiating voice and brown doe-like eyes – a Jew in every respect. 'Oh!' says he, in the oleaginous Semitic way, and accurately taking up his cue (for all this was rehearsed patter), 'my wife says "my face is my fortune".'

'No wonder you're so hard up and 'ave got to take in lodgers. What's yer name?'

'John Jones,' in a demure wheedling voice.

'Hoo – that's not your name in your own bloody country – I expect it's Hullabullinsky.'

'Do you know what my name really is?'

'No.'

'It's Assenheimopoplocatdwizlinsky Kovorod.'

(Loud Laughter.)

'I shall call you "ass" for short.'

I was laughing loudly at these two clowns and the skipper observing as much, shouted out to me:–

'Parlez-vous Français, M'sieur?'

'Oui, oui,' said I.

'Ah! lah, you're one of us – oh! what a game! what a bees' nest,' and all the time he went on selling caps and chucking them at the purchasers.

Perhaps one of the most extraordinary things I saw was a stream of young men who, one after another, came up to a stall, paid a penny and swallowed a glass of 'nerve tonic' – a green liquid syphoned out of a large jar – warranted a safe cure for 'Inward weakness, slightest flurry or body oppressed.'

But I should go on for hours if I were to tell everything seen in this remarkable lane during an hour and a half on a Sunday morning. Each stall-holder sells only one kind of article – caps or clocks or songs, braces, shawls, indecent literature, concertinas, gramophones, coats, pants, reach-me-downs, epergnes. The thoroughfare was crowded with people (I saw two Lascars in red fez caps) inspecting the goods displayed and attentively observed by numerous policemen. The alarm clocks were all going off, each gramophone was working a record (a different one!) and every tradesman shouting his wares – a perfect pandemonium.

Phil May recorded his vision of a cosmopolitan and good-humoured Petticoat Lane, alias Middlesex Street, in 1897.

'W. N. P. Barbellion', 1914

Some typical London costermongers on the way to an exhibition of their donkeys and ponies held at the People's Palace in the Mile End Road (see page 111) in 1892.

Flower girls touting for customers from their base around the Sir Robert Peel memorial at the west end of Cheapside. William Behrens's statue, as dull as its subject, was readily sacrificed to the motor car in 1935, and since 1971 has been suitably housed in the grounds of the police college at Hendon.

ILLEGAL TRADING

In the neighbourhood to which I am referring hundreds of costers with their barrows are to be seen every Sunday morning. If they are an evil, I am convinced they are a necessary one. It is practically impossible for a great many of the East End poor to do all their marketing on a Saturday night. Many a toiler does not leave the workshop of the sweater until after the shops have closed, and of course the wages are not paid until the last stitch has been put in. Again, those who do their work at home are frequently unable to deliver it until the last thing at night. Then it must not be forgotten that the barrow-men, having no rent or taxes to pay, can sell their meat, fish, vegetables, and other commodities at a lower price than the shopkeepers. Moreover, the costers, with their wives and families, form no small portion of the community, and if their occupation were gone, they would go to still further flood the already overflooded labour market.

I am aware that, according to the strict letter of the law, this trading is illegal. Shortly after my visit to Sclater Street, proceedings were taken before me against a number of barrow-men who traded in that locality; but I am happy to say that an amicable arrangement was come to. I paid a special visit to the locality – on the 9th of March, 1889 – to ascertain how far it was correct to say that these costermongers caused an obstruction. I found them quiet and orderly, and it seemed to me that there was very little ground for complaint.

Montagu Williams, 1892

SIR ROBERT'S FLOWER GIRLS

Amongst the army of flower girls are skirmishers who 'advance to the attack.' St. Paul's Churchyard is the skirmishers' paradise. Sir Robert Pell's statue at the western end of Cheapside is their base of operations. They leave their stock around the pedestal while they move about, lynx-eyed, eager, prompt. It requires boundless energy to bring their wares under the eyes of the sprinkling of people in that jostling crowd who are potential purchasers, and need but to be tactfully tempted. There are often as many as nine girls at the statue; but that is only for a minute or two, to replenish their stocks from the reserve. They are quickly off again to the kerbstone.

P. F. William Ryan, 1903

WHERE TO EAT IN THE CITY

A stranger who wants to become acquainted with the City in one of its most strongly-marked peculiarities, ought to be there about noon and take his lunch. The City restaurants are naturally almost exclusively day restaurants, and most of them

are closed at 8 p.m. Almost the whole of their trade is done at lunch time, between the hours of 1 and 3 p.m., but during that time they are truly chock-full of customers, which is not exactly comfortable according to German notions. In many restaurants, especially those frequented by clerks, where a steak may be had for 9d. and potatoes for a penny, the rush of customers is so great that behind our chair there is already another customer who waits for us to make room for him when we have finished. In other restaurants, as at Pimms', the guests stand, or sit on high three-legged stools, before a long bar, with their hats on their heads. Here, too, there is a constant coming and going of customers, who lunch in quickly-changing shifts. To get a whole table for oneself alone in a City restaurant is a very exceptional occurrence. Of late, large up-to-date restaurants planned to cater simultaneously for a very considerable number of guests have been built; for instance, one in Palmerston House, and others by Lyons & Co., etc. Frequently the restaurants are subterranean, several floors below each other, to which access is gained by lifts. In such cases everything is, of course, lighted by electricity.

The prices are mostly moderate, according to English notions. For a shilling one can satisfy his appetite with a fairly good meal. Payment is generally made at a desk near the entrance to the place, the waiter handing the customer his bill. Compared with Continental restaurants, the product of the sea – such as oysters, lobsters, crabs, and all sorts of sea fish – figures very largely on the bills of fare. But the real *pièce de résistance* is always the grilled steak or chop. The principal fish restaurants in the City are the various branches of Pimms' and Sweetings'.

Among other large restaurants I may mention the Guildhall Tavern, Palmerston House, Lyons & Co., City Arms, etc. German restaurants are also numerously represented. One may have meals *à l'Allemande* at Kohler's in Coleman Street (in the Wool Exchange); at the Loewenbraeu, in Gracechurch Street; at Burger's, in Cullum Street; at Goetze's, in Coleman Street, and in many other places.

The usual drinks are bitter ale and stout, whiskey and soda, or lager beer. Champagne or wine is but seldom taken. Altogether, moderation is predominant, owing to the necessity of keeping the head cool for the afternoon's work. Characteristic of the tendency of modern life is the fact that temperance restaurants, though rapidly multiplying in the City, are always overcrowded. Slater's, Lyons' tea-shops, the A B C, offer food to the cautious mortal who has adopted the principle of not taking alcohol before his evening meal. Good food is given for little money and washed down with a glass of water or lemonade.

Carl Peters, 1904

. . . AND IN THE WEST END

While the more ancient taverns of Covent Garden and of the City have largely lost their fashionable vogue, the general improvement in restaurants and modern hotels has been rapid. In the last twenty years, revolutions have been worked in this

Old fashioned City catering still dominated Warwick Square, behind the Old Bailey, as the nineteenth century ended. These long-vanished establishments were West's Dining Rooms and the Three Jolly Butchers.

A West End restaurant in 1895. The family in the foreground are surely discussing dress allowances.

respect. Twenty years ago, to begin with small things, a cup of tea at a confectioner's cost at least sixpence, and was not always easy to get; now, it is obtainable for two or three pence anywhere, and for a penny at cheap shops. Everything else in the commissariat has improved and cheapened in proportion. Elegant little dinners may be had now at all prices; from the famous 'Savoy' dinner at a guinea, to the cheap and dainty repast 'in the Italian style' at 2s. 6d. Of this latter class is the 'Comedy' Restaurant, Panton Street, in a small and hidden by-way, where little dinners, comprising smart waiters, separate tables, candle-shades, and table decorations, are provided for the modest price of half-a-crown per head. Or at the Holborn Restaurant Dinner, at 3s. 6d., you may, if so inclined, enjoy the strains of a band, while entertaining your pre-theatre party. Or, if you be rich, the big hall of the new and expensive 'Carlton' is now the most modish place for after-theatre supper parties. Here the parting guest is politely 'sped', if he linger, by lamps discreetly and suggestively lowered at intervals. . . . Ah, what a delightful city London is for the rich to live in! Everything may be had and enjoyed!

The Art, then, even the Poetry, of Dining, may be thoroughly studied in London at the present day. Every passing mood may be consulted, every gastronomic fancy indulged. You may choose your company as you choose your *menu*; you may make a free selection from the quality of either. You have but to know exactly beforehand what you want. If the lady whom you honour be frivolous by nature, you can take her to the smart restaurant of the Hotel Bristol, and to a comedy adapted 'from the French'; if she be serious, to the 'Grand Hotel', and then to Shakespeare; if crude, to Frascati's and to melodrama. But, whether you choose expensive dining places or cheap ones, and in whatever manner you may elect to spend your long London day, one thing is certain, that at its close you will generally find yourself to have spent a considerable sum. For, howe'er improved and reformed, in essentials the city is yet not much changed since the days of John Lydgate, who found, he says, to his cost, and even so early as the fifteenth century that:

'lacking mony I mighte not spede.'

Mrs. E. T. Cook, 1902

Chapter 7

THE DAILY GRIND

The history of the City of London can be best understood as a continuous process of specialisation. Once it housed all the people and all their work. The first change was the squeezing out of the poor, who had to live in the suburbs. The rich eventually followed their example, but moved in a different direction. Then industry departed to more spacious quarters, and before long most of the shops migrated west. In the last decades of the nineteenth century the decline of the Port of London meant that the need for warehouses was lessening. It was becoming clear that soon only the offices would be left, and by 1900 the clerk was very much the representative City worker. In the West End servants, shop assistants and waiters were more prominent, but even here the growth of bureaucracy was giving work to an army of clerks.

London's position as a manufacturing city was under threat from both home and foreign competition. Although this was then almost as great a worry to politicians as her commercial decline, we are now in a position to see it as an unmixed blessing. The long drift of industry to the provinces via the suburbs has helped to keep the congestion of London's streets just within bounds, and has contributed immensely to reducing the pollution of her air and river.

There has also been a moral gain, or perhaps rather a gain in morale, for it meant that London had a comparatively short exposure to the worst aspects of the factory system. We owe this to the squeezing out of industry that began late in the nineteenth century, just at the time when the minute sub-division of work in factories was being introduced under American influence. It inevitably produced the malaise against which Ruskin and his followers warned, 'the modern view of labour – a view which regards it as an irksome, and narrowing, and unlovely thing'. Fortunately the huge buildings required for the full development of this system could rarely be squeezed into the crowded and immensely valuable streets of London.

The city had a longer experience of the evils of home and workshop industry, where the sweating system flourished, especially in the East End and in Soho. It was defined in 1903 as "an unhappy combination of long hours and low pay. 'The sweater's den' is a workshop – often a dwelling room as well – in which, under the most unhealthy conditions, men and women toil for from sixteen to eighteen hours a day for a wage barely sufficient to keep body and soul together." Tailoring and bootmaking were the classic sweated trades, and in the East End (where there were more than two thousand such workshops in 1900) exploited and exploiter were very often immigrant Jews from Russia, Poland and Roumania.

Rush hour in Fleet Street c. 1895, and not a woman in sight. The Ludgate Hill railway bridge is in the distance.

LONDON'S GOD

London is the chief abode of the great god Money, whose throne, visible to all men, is in the heart of the City. From Queen Street and Guildhall to Gracechurch Street and Bishopsgate, from London Bridge to London Wall, lies a region in which the temples of the god cluster together in thick profusion. From there the greatest and the most numerous of his activities are conducted; for London, in spite of the rivalry of New York and the growing importance of Paris and Berlin as money centres, is still paramount as a headquarters of exchange and banking.

In the banking section of the 'Post Office Directory' there are over 11,000 entries informing the inquirer as to the banking representation in London of practically every town in the world. With few exceptions all these references are contained in the section of London I have indicated. A walk through the miles of streets and lanes in this quarter will not fail to reveal to the observer the vast importance of London in this respect. All the buildings, save for a sprinkling of restaurants, churches, and shops, are banks of one kind and another, insurance offices, loan agencies, offices of mortgage brokers, foreign merchants, stock and share brokers, bullion dealers, insurance brokers, investment agents, assayers, and the like.

Our faith, prompted by the traditions of the place and the sight of leagues of palatial offices, not to mention multitudes of most expensively dressed City gentlemen, begins dimly to understand that this is indeed the abode of the god Money. But it is not long before the god himself appears. We are outside a well-known joint-stock bank. A vehicle resembling a private omnibus drives up. This is the car of the god. His mightiness is heralded by a shrill whistle. Attendants appear, and, without ceremony, the god is handed in bags from one to another on his way to the bank's strong room somewhere in the basement. We hear the words 'All gold', 'All silver', or 'All copper', passed from one official to the next – whether facetiously or by rule does not appear. We were beginning to think that money existed here only in an intangible form, that it was all a matter of figures in books, standing for something far away and unrealisable, and that at the best there might be a profusion of cheques and bills of exchange. On the contrary, in this region there probably is at any time a greater amount of gold than anywhere else in the world. The Bank of England alone has always some thirty-five millions in bullion, and frequently more, a mass of gold on which the credit of the country in certain last contingencies depends. By the way, a million pounds in gold weighs about eight tons.

Charles Turner, 1903

PORTUGUESE THREES

It was with a certain uneasiness that I crossed Throgmorton Street and entered the forbidden precincts, elbowing through the close throng around me. I went up the doorsteps to the ant-hill of people profoundly contrite at being poor, a son of a very poor country, even bankrupt publicly. Admittance was a great proof of favour, because the Stock Exchange only admits members, but rarely visitors. The chairman who took me through, said to me meaningly, 'It is two years since a stranger was admitted.' I felt confused when I had passed the door; in this place must have been the golden calf that the Jews so offended by worshipping in a moment of reactionary piety. It has an enormous roof surmounted by a dome. Around are deep chapels, and in each a pulpit with a priest in scarlet vestments by the side of a board where the quotations

The superb banking hall of Prescott, Dimsdale, Cave, Tugwell & Co. at 50 Cornhill sketched soon after it opened for business in 1892. The firm was eventually absorbed into the National Provincial Bank, which had a branch here for many years, but the building (little altered) is now the Counting House pub.

The Stock Exchange taking a break from business to celebrate some rare good news from South Africa, the surrender of General Cronjé, in February 1900.

are marked in chalk. Columns of polished marble sustain the dome, through which the light enters abundantly.

There is a vague hum of thousands of men who rush about, get into groups, and take notes in pocket-books, but all quietly, without that hateful and hellish row of the public Bourse of Paris. Nothing of this here. The company owning the house possesses a capital of £240,000 in 20,000 shares of £12 each. To be admitted one has to find security. There are three kinds of members: the first, with three securities, pay £525; the second, with two, pay £157 10s.; and thirdly the clerks, if 'authorised' pay £52 10s., and if unauthorised, £10 10s. Beyond this there is no admittance. The public wait at the doors, as the people did in the days of the old Spanish Councils. Outside there is another kind of noise, nervously hurried 'tips' and information, and audible remarks on those who enter the sacred precincts.

Inside, each set has its own chapel, its ritual, and its place in which gather the different orders of the priests of the Calf. The entire world is represented there, either by nations or species of business. Here are public funds, there are mines, there shipping companies, there railways, there factories. Here is the metropolis, there are the United States, elsewhere are Brazil or Australia, the entire world, without omitting a poor corner of it in which I saw with compunction that they were dealing in 'Portuguese Threes'. My soul fell on its feet.

To be poor, weak, and insignificant is a dishonour in this land of Darwin, that has hoisted the victory of England in the life-and-death competition of this age as the flag of universal science; while the poor, and the weak, and the lowly, and the humble often conquer also, according to the Gospel for

which the English seriously imagine they have so profound a veneration. It will be understood that, situated as I was under the weight of these impressions, the great sight of the turn of the engine of the world's riches produced in me an unpleasing effect.

Oliveira Martins, 1894

IMPERTINENT PERSONALITIES

The street cries of London (at least in its more polite circles) are much diminished in intensity. Even the muffin man's bell, so welcome in the winter afternoon's gloom, seems now more seldom heard. 'Sweet Lavender,' however, still has a familiar autumn sound, and the flower-hawkers of spring are still discordant. Yet one's ears are no longer so generally deafened, and the reason for this is not far to seek. For London is now so gay with advertisements that in every direction our eyes meet strange, gaily-coloured hoarding and sky signs; and the manifold attractions of various articles, instead of being cried in the streets, now cry at us from the walls, or shout discordantly at us from out of the blue of heaven, from ugly black wires and glaring brazen letters. We cannot go out of doors without being asked a hundred times, in varying type, such silly questions as 'Why does a Woman Look Old Sooner than a Man?' 'Why Let Your Baby Die?' 'Why Pay House Rent?' or other such idiotic queries. Why, who *would* pay house rent, especially in London, if he or she could help it? In shops, or on railways, it is the same. For at least several miles out of

A representative range of advertisements on display in Southampton Row in 1903, when the street was being widened as part of the Aldwych and Kingsway development.

London you travel in the constant company of 'Pear's Soap', and 'Colman's Mustard'; and outside eating-shops you see in large letters the cunning legend, 'Everything as Nice as Mother Makes it.' The Art of Advertisement is everywhere paramount. You cannot even travel in the humble omnibus without being implored 'not to let your wife worry over the house-cleaning,' and being asked 'why your nose gets red after eating'; together with suggested remedies for both these sad states of things. These are really, when one comes to think of it, impertinent personalities. This mania for posters has, of course, largely resulted from the modern spread of education: for of what use to ask such questions in old days, when few could have succeeded in reading them? The fashion of advertisements is still growing, the Americans are encouraging it to preposterous proportions; and we shall soon, indeed, live in a mere criss-cross of lettered wires, not unlike Mr. Wells's idea of a future Utopia.

Mrs. E. T. Cook, 1902

THE LAST CIRCLE OF THE INFERNO

Work at the docks is the last refuge for the shipwrecked of society. He who has never seen a multitude of the miserable crowding round the gates every morning, begging an alms in the shape of a day's work, has never got an intimate notion of what misfortune there is in the world, or of the extravagance at the top of society resulting from the contrast of the social elements. A Dante in our times would place scenes of this kind in the last circle of his Inferno.

There hovers in the air an atmosphere of vice, one breathes the full acrid fume of miserable dirtiness, one sees the foul rags and tatters of civilised life. The multitude of pariahs come from every part; there are sons of the soil whose arms the unkind earth rejects; there are town lads who have gone under in the strife of unseemly competition; there are bankrupt shop-keepers, workmen out of employ, old soldiers, clerks, all classes, mingled in the hunger that makes all alike, amid a dense multitude of drunken vagabonds from the quarters of the East End, like repulsive savages, with downcast

Bitumen being unloaded for A. Grimwood & Co., of Victoria Street, at Limehouse. This was Elizabeth Wharf, Dupont Street, on the Regent's Canal, not far north of what is now Limehouse Basin.

eyes, scarred flesh, ragged clouts, in the hope of earning some pence at carrying loads in order afterwards to spend the money in making beasts of themselves in the gin palace in the Commercial Road.

Oliveira Martins, 1894

SYMBOLIC SQUALOR

I find an irresistible charm in any sort of river-navigation, but I scarce know how to speak of the little voyage from Westminster Bridge to Greenwich. It is in truth the most prosaic possible form of being afloat, and to be recommended rather to the inquiring than to the fastidious mind. It initiates you into the duskiness, the blackness, the crowdedness, the intensely commercial character of London. Few European cities have a finer river than the Thames, but none certainly has expended more ingenuity in producing a sordid river-front. For miles and miles you see nothing but the sooty

backs of warehouses, or perhaps they are the sooty faces: in buildings so utterly expressionless it is impossible to distinguish. They stand massed together on the banks of the wide turbid stream, which is fortunately of too opaque a quality to reflect the dismal image. A damp-looking, dirty blackness is the universal tone. The river is almost black, and is covered with black barges; above the black housetops, from among the far-stretching docks and basins, rises a dusky wilderness of masts. The little puffing steamer is dingy and gritty – it belches a sable cloud that keeps you company as you go. In this carboniferous shower your companions, who belong chiefly, indeed, to the classes bereft of lustre, assume an harmonious grayness; and the whole picture, glazed over with the glutinous London mist, becomes a masterly composition. But it is very impressive in spite of its want of lightness and brightness, and though it is ugly it is anything but trivial. Like so many of the aspects of English civilisation that are untouched by elegance or grace, it has the merit of expressing something very serious. Viewed in this intellectual light the polluted river, the sprawling barges, the dead-faced

The Pool of London c. 1890, when the Monument and the tower of St Magnus the Martyr were easily the tallest landmarks on the north bank. The most conspicuous was Billingsgate Market, on the right.

warehouses, the frowsy people, the atmospheric impurities become richly suggestive. It sounds rather absurd, but all this smudgy detail may remind you of nothing less than the wealth and power of the British Empire at large; so that a kind of metaphysical magnificence hovers over the scene, and supplies what may be literally wanting. I don't exactly understand the association, but I know that when I look off to the left at the East India Docks, or pass under the dark hugely piled bridges, where the railway trains and the human processions are for ever moving, I feel a kind of imaginative thrill. The tremendous piers of the bridges, in especial, seem the very pillars of the Empire aforesaid.

Henry James, 1877

BEETLING WAREHOUSES

The charm of exploring the City is ever novel – to me at least. Not every one has thoroughly fallen under the spell; for an occasional visit is not enough. One should linger, and come again and explore, and be led hither and thither by the humour and attraction of the moment. At the different seasons of the day, morning, noon, and evening – nay, on the Sunday even, when it becomes an astounding wilderness – it

offers quite different aspects, and a succession of surprises. It is in truth another city, another people, we never can get rid of the notion that we are entering a foreign town. Often has been described the aspect of the overwhelming tide of busy men, all hurrying and crowding and pushing past at a brisk speed; the carriages, waggons, carts, incessantly moving in a crowded procession; the hum and roar in the ears. The vast size, solidity, and imposing stateliness of the buildings astonish us. But more pleasing is the picturesque irregularity, and windings and curves of the bye-streets or alleys, changed by the tall and massive structures which line them into Genoa-like streets, lacking only the *grilles* and the gloom. Here is the contrast to the West End; and here is seen the different spirit which animates the merchant, as compared with the smaller trader. *His* ideas are magnificent: he must have his trading palace and warehouses beetling, lofty, and of granite or Portland stone, a great arch or portal for the entrance; a sort of City architecture has been engendered specially to meet his wants.

Most 'West-enders' rarely travel beyond the Exchange and the banking streets adjoining. But until Cornhill is passed, this peculiar aspect we have been describing is not met with. It is when we reach Mincing Lane, and Mark Lane, and Leadenhall, and Fenchurch Street, that we come upon these grand and endless ranges of business palaces. Sometimes, as in

the case of Fenchurch Court, the greater thoroughfares are joined by a long paved footway, lined with these vast storied buildings. It seems a bit of Brussels city; the office windows, it may be, looking out upon a small patch of churchyard, allowed to linger on in a grudging way. This irregularity is often as surprising as it is picturesque; witness that fine, massively pillared doorway, last fragment of some noble mansion, which is the entrance to a descending covered way, leading first to a tavern and thence into Leadenhall Street. It is in these imposing alleys that we come upon some conventual-looking City Hall, its great gates closed, its windows forlorn-looking, and barred like some disused monastery.

Percy Fitzgerald, 1890

THE GREAT FIRE IN THE CITY

At two o'clock on the afternoon of Friday, Nov.19, the greatest fire since 1666 broke out in Hamsell Street, Aldersgate Street, and spread with alarming rapidity through six or seven streets, completely gutting the houses over many acres of ground, and doing incalculable damage to property. For five solid hours the efforts of the Fire Brigade, strenuous

A typical Victorian building of the eastern City, with a shop on the ground floor, office on the first, and warehouse above. The surprise about 14 Cree Church Lane is to discover that it survives, cranes and all, very little altered.

Not the Blitz, but the devastation after the great Jewin Street fire of 1897. The area was rapidly rebuilt, only for almost exactly similar scenes to be repeated in 1941. The Barbican Estate is now on the site.

and magnificent though they were, could do nothing towards checking the fury of the flames, which blazed furiously until long after nightfall. By midnight, however, the fire was got in hand, but not until nearly three hundred warehouses in Hamsell Street, Well Street, Jewin Street, Jewin Crescent, Monkswell Street, Australian Avenue, and Redcross Street had been burnt to the ground. The district is the centre of the feather trade, and the headquarters of dealers in light fancy goods, so that the fire did not lack for food of the most easily inflammable nature. Tie-manufacturers, skin and fur merchants, umbrella-makers, straw bonnet-makers, mantle-makers, New Zealand merchants and importers of foreign fancy wares have sustained losses which will in the aggregate amount to nearly a million sterling. It is said that the great destruction of this year's stock of hat-feathers will materially increase the price of these luxuries (or are they necessities?) during the coming season. The insurance risk is borne by nearly every British fire company.

Among buildings of interest in the neighbourhood, the only one that suffered was the old Grapes tavern, which was completely destroyed. For a time it was feared that the ancient church of St Giles, Cripplegate, must be consumed, and every spectator of antiquarian sympathies was concerned for the safety of the historic church, which escaped the Great Fire. St Giles's, indeed, dates from the time of William Rufus. In it Cromwell was married, Fox and Milton were buried. For a time the roof of the church was actually ablaze, but the firemen succeeded in saving the building from serious damage. Damage by water there is certainly, and the church services will for a little be interrupted. Milton's tomb is adorned with an elegant sculptured miniature of the poet,

and this has fortunately escaped injury. The Grinling Gibbons carving, too, remains intact. The fire happening in the daytime, and in a confined space, afforded less 'spectacle' than would otherwise have been the case; but the few who contrived, as the evening descended, to obtain a general view of the scene from the tower of St Giles's declare that the conflagration, although by that time past its first fierceness, was impressive and memorable.

'Illustrated London News' Nov.27, 1897

BARGAIN HUNTERS

Here this Saturday afternoon in Smithfield, now that more than half the stalls are shut, comes a staid, matured City clerk with his shrewd, economical little wife and their eldest son, a dapper youth who has himself just become 'something in the City' and has met them by arrangement, but reluctantly, and in some fear of compromising his budding dignity. Depend upon it, the matured clerk has a large family, or they take in boarders to eke out his salary. The inevitable men, women, and children who hover about the gates to sell penny canvas or straw bags know them by sight as regular Saturday customers, and their experience stands them in good stead.

They do nothing rashly. Having inspected a dozen stalls, they go back to one they had passed, and secure a shoulder of mutton or a great piece of beef for remarkably little money. At the newer end of the Market, where they have now and then picked up a bargain in poultry, they buy several pounds of good cheap bacon and a formidable wedge of cheese.

The London Central Market, seen here in 1905, was built as a replacement for the ancient open-air Smithfield to the south. It began trading in 1868, and was extended several times before the end of the century. This is Long Lane at its meeting with West Smithfield.

Sir Horace Jones, who designed the Temple Bar griffin, was also responsible for the rebuilding of Billingsgate Market between 1874 and 1877. This is the river frontage, c. 1905. Porters carried the boxes of fish up the iron bridges from boat to dock.

Then they go out and across the road to the Fish and Vegetable Market, where they get some fish for this evening's dinner or supper, and lay in a stock of fruit and tomatoes, supplemented by a selection of marrows and, possibly, a couple of cucumbers; so that, at last, when they shape their course for a penny tramcar home, the clerk is carrying two bags, his wife has her arms full of miscellanies, and their son, following them with a hang-dog, furtive air, eyes the passers-by loweringly, and, with the bag of shamelessly protruding meat in one hand and the basket of fish in the other, is secretly praying he may not be seen by anybody who knows him.

Arthur Rutland, 1901

A MORNING AT BILLINGSGATE

If you go round to the front of the Market, even as late as a quarter to five this summer morning, there is little or no life at all in Lower Thames Street; but just before the hour sounds from the neighbouring steeples a clatter of hoofs and grinding of wheels on the stony road jar through the stillness, and a ponderous railway van, heavily burdened, sweeps down Fish Street Hill and pulls up gallantly opposite the yet closed gates of the Market. You hear a similar van rattling after it; and nearer, making more sedate haste along Thames Street, glides a private brougham, which stops at the door of one of the crazy, tumbledown old fish shops, and a substantial, prosperous-looking merchant alights with a cigar in his mouth, and, calling a 'Good-morning, Thomas,' to the

coachman, who touches his hat and drives off, lets himself in with a latchkey. You may see him presently, when his shutters are down, disguised in a white smock and a cloth cap, writing at his desk among trickling consignments of newly arrived fish and shouting lustily to perspiring assistants.

Directly Billingsgate unfastens its gates the streets in its vicinity are all alive. It is as if some wizard haunting the deserted spot muttered a cabalistic word, and, hey, presto! public-houses and coffee-houses are wide open; shops of fish salesmen and factors on Fish Street Hill, St. Mary-at-Hill, and Thames Street are stripped of their shutters, and high-packed vehicles, mysteriously materialised, are lining the kerbs before them; the two railway vans outside the Market are rapidly multiplying into so many that the roadway is getting impassable; fish porters innumerable hurtle, as it were, from the clouds and up from the earth, as if every paving-stone were a trap-door, and swarming everywhere in white smocks and round, iron-hard hats, designed to cushion heavy burdens, are deftly unloading all the carts. There are continuous processions of such porters trotting into the Market with oozy, trickling boxes on their heads, and there are continuous processions trotting out of the Market, handing metal tallies to the carters by way of receipts, hoisting fresh boxes on to their heads, and joining one or other of the processions trotting in.

If you pass through the cool, dim, sloppy Market and out on to the wooden platform at the rear, you see the steamers here being unloaded in like manner. A broad iron bridge slopes down to them, and down one side of the bridge porters are hurrying empty-handed, and up the other side porters stream one after the other with boxes on their heads, lidless boxes crusted with ice that is melting and dribbling through on the bearers.

By this, the interior of the Market has lost its barren look. The stalls, each of which is merely a desk and a floor space, are becoming congested with stacks of boxes; with barrels of eels, and barrels and loose mountains of lobsters, mussels, whelks; with salmon and cod ranged on the stones or on raised boards, or, in the shops that occupy the two sides of the Market, on shiny, slippery slabs. There are bloaters from Yarmouth; there are kippers from Peterhead and Stornoway; there are all manner of fish from Hull, Grimsby, Milford Haven, Fleetwood – all manner of places round the British Isles that have any fish to send anywhere seem to have sent them here.

The bustling and shouting increase until by half-past six, or thereabouts, the tide of business is at the full, and beginning to turn. The railway vans have gone, and other railway and carriers' and fishmongers' carts that have been hovering in Eastcheap and other outlying streets, and the costers who have been clustering their barrows at the lower end of Love Lane, are swooping in to bargain and buy, or to carry away consignments of fish already ordered, and the Market is emptying as rapidly as it filled.

Noon is not more than two hours gone when Billingsgate is practically shut again; the fish shops round about look as if they had been looted by an invading army; fish porters lounge at street corners, or in public-houses and coffee-shops, and vast-booted men tramp clumsily inside the Market and in front of it, trailing snaky hoses and washing the stones.

Arthur Rutland, 1901

DIRT AND THE PICTURESQUE

At Blackfriars, the Victoria Embankment ends, and tall, many-storied warehouses crowd down to the water's edge, in picturesque though dingy medley, with, behind them, the blackened dome of St. Paul's, attended by its sentinel spires, – St. Paul's, that has nearly all the way stood out prominently in the distance, making this, by universal consent, the finest view in all London. The noble effect of Wren's great work is indeed, apparently from all points; but it is the river and the wharves that, no doubt, form its best and most fitting foreground. As we near London Bridge, the dirt of the vast highway gains upon us; but, it must be confessed, its general picturesqueness is thereby immeasurably increased. Dirt, after

The view up Fish Street Hill towards the Monument, c. 1910. The Steam Packet, a pub much patronised by Billingsgate porters, was at 128 Lower Thames Street. It has been displaced, like nearly everything else on the left, by Regis House.

all, is always so near akin to picturesqueness. The mud-banks and the mud become more constant, the bustle and hum of the great city are everywhere evident. Barges are moored under the tall warehouses; workmen stand in the storing-places above, hauling up the goods from the boats with ropes and pulleys; it is a scene of ceaseless activity, an activity too, which increases as you descend the stream. On the one side, the slums and warehouses of Upper Thames Street; on the other, the yet slummier purlieus of busy, often-burned-down Tooley Street. Thames Street, like its adjoining Billingsgate, is, I may remark, nearly always muddy, whatever the time of year. On rainy days, it is like a Slough of Despond. If by chance you wish to land at All Hallows or London Bridge Piers, you must first climb endless wooden and slippery steps, then wend your way carefully past threatening cranes, and along narrow alleys between high houses, alleys blocked by heavy waggons, from which tremendous packages ascend, by rope, to top stories; alleys where there is barely room for a solitary pedestrian to wedge himself past the obstruction. Barrels of the delicious oyster, the obnoxious 'cockle', the humble 'winkle'; loud scents that suggest the immediate neighbourhood of the ubiquitous 'kipper'; these, mingled with the shouts of fish-wives and porters, greet you near that Temple of the Fisheries, Billingsgate. The enormous Monument, which stands close by, may be said to be in the dirtiest, dingiest portion of this dingy region. 'Fish Street Hill' the locality is called; and it certainly is no misnomer.

Mrs. E. T. Cook, 1902

A REMARKABLE SCENE

The scene in this market in the early morning is a remarkable one, full of activity and bustle. It is worth a visit even in the winter months, and especially on Christmas Eve, but it is in summer, during the height of the fruit and flower season, that it is seen at its best.

As we approach the market in the early dawn of a summer's morning we find most of the adjoining streets filled with carts. Formerly the streets were well nigh impassable even for foot-passengers, but owing to the clearances lately made, both on the side of Bow Street and of Henrietta Street, there is now good standing ground for the larger part of the carts in the market itself. Still, even now we sometimes have to creep under a cart to make our way across the street, and vehicular traffic is of course an impossibility. Under the porch of St. Paul's Church an old man is selling a curious but much patronized concoction of eels in water. This mixture does not look inviting, so we politely decline his invitation to refresh ourselves, and pass on. At Lockhart's Coffee Tavern, under the Piazza, where a roaring trade is proceeding, we regale ourselves with a good cup of coffee and a roll. The shops in the Central Avenue are not yet open, and the auctions in the Floral Hall do not begin till much later, but the side avenues are filled with fruit and vegetable sellers, and the Flower Market is in all its glory. Few sights can be prettier than the one it presents when it first opens in the morning in summer. Brilliant flowers of all hues and kinds are ranged upon the stands, while the rising sun lights up the whole scene. The agents and foremen of the different shops in the

The Bedford Hotel, part of which was once the Bedford Coffee House, favourite haunt of writers and actors, stood at the north-eastern corner of Covent Garden, between Russell Street and the Floral Hall. The photograph was taken shortly before the hotel and this part of the 'piazza' were sacrificed to make more room for the market in 1887–8.

market are hurrying from stand to stand, buying the flowers that they think will sell. They enter their purchases, prices, &c., in small note-books which are provided on the spot by hawkers of such wares. There is an old man in the market who goes about with a heap of note-books for sale for 3*d*. He has done this business in the market for twenty years, and makes, we should say, judging from the amount of his custom, a good thing out of it. We wend our way along with some difficulty, having to keep our wits about us to avoid the porteresses carrying their big baskets of flowers, and the porters with baskets heaped up one above the other on their heads. Sometimes a collision or a stumble causes these baskets to fall, and as they are laden they not unfrequently give severe bruises to the unwary passer-by. Here and there we come upon a collector gathering the tolls, or a sub-collector or inspector remonstrating with someone who is infringing the rules of the market. Busy as the scene is, we are struck by the good temper and good humour apparent on all sides. At about 8 o'clock the shops on the centre avenue are beginning to take down their shutters. By this time the stands in the Flower Market are nearly denuded of flowers, most of which have been already bought. At 8.30 a warning bell is rung, for at 9 a.m. the buyers must leave the Flower Market. If anyone attempts to linger after that hour, he is hustled out by the police. Towards closing time we have been perpetually asked by the stand-keepers if we will not buy this or that flower, and we have always returned from our matutinal visits to the market, with one, two, or three pots presented to us by our friends from the stock they have been unable to sell.

The work of the people in the market is hard enough, as may be gathered from the account of a day given by a shop foreman. In winter he gets to work at 5 a.m., and in summer at 3.30 a.m.; he buys and sells in the Flower Market till 9 a.m., when he goes to his shop in the centre avenue; he works there till 8 in the evening, unless, indeed, he has to do the decorations for a ball or some other festivity. When royalty goes to the theatres in the neighbourhood he has to take flowers there for them, such flowers being paid for by the theatre people.

E. C. Grey, 1891

A BUSY COUNTRY TOWN

The long stretch of road which leads out of London by Whitechapel and Bow offers some interesting surprises. Thus we pass through Whitechapel of a market-day, to find the whole street up and down quite blocked up by the enormous waggons and carts of compressed hay offered for sale; while rustics in smocks stand round – the whole suggesting a busy country town. In the broad Whitechapel Road we see the old and the new side by side; spacious marts next to old tiled 'hunched' houses; a highly picturesque square of almshouses, somewhat suggesting the condemned Emmanuel Hospital at Westminster.

Percy Fitzgerald, 1893

Whitechapel High Street, the City's hay market, in 1899. The coffee tavern at the corner of New Castle Street (now Tyne Street) is still a café one hundred years later.

SADLY RESPECTABLE

The friend who had invited me to this spectacle felt its inadequacy so keenly, in spite of my protests, that he questioned the policemen for some very squalid or depraved purlieu that he might show me, for we were in the very heart of Whitechapel, but failing that, because the region had been so very much reformed and cleaned up since the dreadful murders there, he had no recourse but to take me on top of a tram-car and show me how very thoroughly it had been reformed and cleaned up. In a ride the whole length of Whitechapel Road to where the once iniquitous region ceased from troubling and rose in a most respectable resurrection as Stepney, with old-fashioned houses which looked happy, harmless homes, I could only be bidden imagine avenues of iniquity branching off on either hand. But I actually saw nothing slumlike; indeed, with a current of cool east wind in our faces, which the motion of the tram reinforced, the ride was an experience delightful to every sense. It was significant also of the endlessness of London that as far as the tram-car took us we seemed as far as ever from the bounds of the city; whatever point we reached there was still as much or more London beyond.

William Dean Howells, 1905

THE SWEETS OF BETHNAL GREEN

Passing the carpenter's shop for box-making, we return to the main building, where we make the acquaintance of what may be called the sweetest aspect of the manufactory. It is the jujube and lozenge department. The first thing one notices is the 'Pâte de guimauve' pan, a remarkable arrangement, whereby it revolves, and at the same time an automatic paddle keeps the luscious ingredients in a constant but regular agitation. From a brown compound the guimauve gradually becomes of a snowy whiteness. In this room glycerine, voice, delectable, magnum bonum, tamarind, and other jujubes are being made. The syrups of fresh fruits are used, and in some cases the fruits themselves. The baker is a Frenchman, looking quite oriental in his fez and white blouse. Other adjacent rooms are occupied with the jujube manufacture. The mixture is poured into flat moulds. These are dried in a long range of rooms, some hot, others cold, all of them artificially ventilated, several with steam fans. When dry the flat sheets are passed through machines which cut them into strips and then into their ordinary sizes. They pass another process of drying, and are then collected and sent to the packing room. The pastilles go through a somewhat different process. They are moulded. Hundreds of cases, prepared by girls, are filled with starch. Over these are passed indenters, and into the moulds the material is poured from tins, which the girls use with remarkable facility. The pastilles are then carried to the drying closets; thence they go to a room in which a number of girls are engaged with long strips of wood bristling with pins. They look like rows of gems or brooches. The starch powder adheres to them, however, here and there.

Women employees of Allen and Hanbury's pharmaceutical factory at Bethnal Green, in their 'aesthetic' uniforms, moulding starch for jujubes in 1892.

From the pinning room they go to the washing room, where they are soused into vats of cold water, coming through this ordeal bright and shining. Once more they are dried, again dipped and dried, and then they pass to a room where the wooden apparatus is pushed through a little machine that strips them and deposits the pastilles in baskets ready for the packers. The men and women employed in the works have separate apartments and distinct duties; in some departments the women wear a uniform dress of white material. Fresh, healthy-looking girls, they are dressed in a somewhat aesthetic gown that gives free play to the limbs and is belted at the waist, the cap being of the same material as the dress.

Joseph Hatton, 1892

THE DEATH SHOP

You take train from Cannon Street, which is due east, beyond St. Paul's, and, by and by, after passing through the sordid lower river outskirts of London, you come to a grimy station labelled Woolwich Arsenal. Here you get out of the train, and inquire of Thomas Atkins, of the Artillery, the way to the Arsenal. When he has pointed out the road, you wend your way by one or two narrow streets to a great brick gateway, guarded by policemen, to whom you deliver up the little ticket from the War Office, which vouches for you as a British subject. And then you are in the Death Shop.

You are in the place where they concentrate death, pack it up into all sorts of shapes and sizes of pills, and export it to the ends of the earth, there to be distributed for the glory of England and the physicking of her enemies. Before you shall have finally departed in the twilight you will realise how many forms the violent variety of death may take. You will come away wondering whether man's proper study is, not so much man, as the means of obliterating and exterminating him. You will be sick with the ingenuity of his schemes of

A scene in the pot fines brass foundry at the Woolwich Arsenal shortly before the Great War.

murder. You will be no less impressed by man's exceeding cleverness than by his diabolical homicidal tendencies.

There are so many ways, so many abrupt and terrible ways, by which death may be administered to our friend the enemy – and you review them so rapidly in a short afternoon at the great Arsenal – that you return to London with only a hazy and confused grasp of all that you have seen. But some things remain with you as distinct and tangible recollections, as to the significance of which you may not blind yourself, and of which you will remember a great deal. You will reckon Woolwich Arsenal amongst those things seen which have impressed you.

J. H. M. Abbott, 1905

THE ORDERLY BOYS

In striking contrast to the elegance of the people in the streets appears the street dirt, which is a characteristic feature of London. The town being built upon a lime formation, no really radical remedy for this defect can be supplied by artificial means, although enormous sums are spent on street cleaning (in the City alone more than £50,000 per annum). The dust always settles again very soon. It is that dust which makes it imperative to often change one's linen while rendering hand-washing almost ineffectual. The roadways are throughout excellent. Wood-paving preponderates in the main streets or flat roads of square freestone. Of late asphalt has come much into use. All this is very modern, but not sufficient to overcome the natural difficulties. Dung and other offal are constantly being cleared away by battalions of boys in uniform, who move freely between the crowded vehicular traffic, depositing the offal in boxes specially erected for that purpose on both sides of the street. In the City alone 192 such boys are regularly employed.

Carl Peters, 1904

The rapid decline and fall of horse transport meant ruin for many men: cabbies, coachmen, ostlers, grooms. A little-known addition to this list were the orderly boys, the most humble of public servants, whose dangerous job was to dodge traffic while scooping up horse droppings. It is hard to see what other employment this could prepare them for, unless possibly the Army.

Chapter 8

TRANSPORT AND COMMUTING

The Utopian forecasters who abounded in 1900 were most comically wide of the mark when they came to consider transport. The wise future, they felt sure, would abolish noise, pollution and delay. For the happy citizens of the twentieth century traffic jams would be a folk memory of quaint Victorian inefficiency. A partial exception to this optimism is found in the prophecies of Ford Madox Hueffer, who in one of his more sensible moments could see that 'we are the tyrants of the men to come; where we build roads their feet must tread'. Even so, he expected the twentieth century to evolve a perfect system of transport for London that would enable all its workers to live in the distant Home Counties.

Almost from the moment that parliament sanctioned the untrammelled use of the motor car in 1896 it was universally accepted that the horse world of London was doomed. This great revolution in transport was taken with airy nonchalance, yet it meant the dismantling of a system brought to a high state of perfection over centuries of experiment. Large parts of the town had been built with stables and coachmen's rooms as an integral part of the design, and many thousands earned a living by driving, or feeding, or tending the horses.

The easy prophecy of the disappearance of the horse was not necessarily combined with any conception of the dreadful and enduring blight we would experience as a result of the motor car's triumph. In 1909 Hueffer wrote that 'the motor traffic itself as we now know it may be considered a comparatively negligible factor in any extended view of the future. For it is a guest that must prove very fugitive as the facilities for electric traction grow. Petrol, with its smell, its noise, its vapours, and the horse with his noise and unsanitary traces, will alike vanish from streets that are in any way properly administered.' This belief in the future of electricity as the motive power for road transport might have taken a jolt from the failure of the electric cabs that had a brief career during the late 1890s, but optimism had been restored by the steady success of the electric tram, which replaced the horse-drawn version in the first decade of the twentieth century.

London's surface railway system was nearly complete by 1887. The only important development during this period was the building of the Great Central Railway into Marylebone in the 1890s, with destructive consequences for St John's Wood. It was into the extension, combination and electrification of the Underground that most investment was directed between 1890 and 1906. This unlovely and unloved service is still the nearest we have come to Utopia in London.

The Cambridge Street coal depot, in the wasteland of goods yards, wharves, and gas works north of St Pancras and King's Cross. The area played a vital part in the daily struggle to feed and heat the capital. This is the view from the south end of Cambridge Street, which is now called Camley Street.

A BRIDGE FROM PAST TO FUTURE

The new Tower of London Bridge, which lies on the seaward side of the entrance to the great capital, is verily a mighty symbol of the British Mind. Like that mind it seems in its entirety to be but an embodiment of straight, symmetrical, exquisitely-balanced lines, void of exaggeration or superfluity. It is a sober piece of architecture, eloquently accurate, and expressing the purpose for which it was designed with that distinctness peculiar to all things English. Thus it plays its part in the stirring scene of quays and docks, and the ceaseless activity of one of the greatest ports in the world. No other water could reflect it in all its beauty, as does the thick, and, in spite of the summer skies, never-blue Thames water. Were it stretched across the Seine or Loire it would wound our artistic sense, as does a discord of colours; here it is significant of grandeur, depth.

Now turn your eyes towards the two towers which support its pillars. Observe their square firm outlines, the steeples that crown their summits, their pointed roofs and narrow Gothic windows; one might imagine it the entrance to some fortified town of the Middle Ages, such as may be seen in certain landscapes. And as the lines cross and recross, mingle and intermingle, they seem to conjure up a vision of some heroic past, and to shoot forth out of the water like some huge flowering plant of olden days. We gaze, and the picture becomes complicated. A narrow iron bridge light and slender, like unto fine lace, crosses the abyss and re-unites them at the top, while another, lower down, level with the quays, rises to let the big ships pass, as beneath a triumphal arch. Thus from the stones of the past Modern Architecture bursts boldly forth, creating future monuments. And with such perfect harmony is this enacted that no false note is heard to mar the blending of the Old and New.

Of a truth there are few countries capable of such contrasts, contrasts so peculiarly suited to England. Perhaps it is because no other people unite with that same harmonious force the worship of the Past and the religion of Tradition to the intense love of progress, the keen and never satisfied passion for the Future.

Gabriel Mourey, 1895

RUSH HOUR

At eight o'clock the roar of the City has gathered strength and fulness, approaching the din of noonday. At nine o'clock every man, woman, and child in the Metropolis seems to be going somewhere. Crowds bubble intermittently from the underground stations. 'Busses in endless procession converge upon the Bank. The pavements are black with people. The scene from the Mansion House steps beggars description. You look upon a very maelström of men. They are not only 'going' to business! They seem to be rushing there!

The subterranean corridors of the Bank 'tube' station are alive with people. Here seconds are as minutes – action is so brisk, time so precious. The observer must stand aside as the passengers from the last-arrived electric train crowd to the steps leading to the open air. At the foot of the staircase their ranks open. The very young men spring forward, glad of a chance to make progress without being rude; the rest climb upward stolidly. In summer some of the men wear straw hats and flannels, some light-coloured tweeds. Many are in the conventional garb, 'spick and span', as though it were afternoon in Piccadilly. What catches the eye is the white of collars and wristbands, and the shine of well-varnished boots. A woman's ungloved hand, heavily ringed, compels you to look at her. She is a middle-aged lady, almost richly, but quietly dressed. You guess her to be a postal official. She has the easy air of the woman of assured income. Yet in her face there is something of the exile's sadness, perhaps because in the autumn of life she is far from woman's natural home.

Tower Bridge nearing completion, viewed from the north bank, probably in 1893.

Weary City and Fleet Street workers plodding homeward across Blackfriars bridge, c. 1905.

A crowded 'bus invites a glance. It is one of the expresses that run between nine and ten every week-day from various suburbs to the City. There is the driver, clean and ruddy, with brown leather gloves, just a somewhat cheap edition of the men who tool their four-in-hands to Hurlingham. Most of the men on top ride every morning from terminus to terminus. In the hot days there are a good many Panama hats and tweed suits. If the weather were less tropical, the prevailing tone would be black, irreproachably black. The men have a Stock Exchange air about them. Many of them no doubt are clerks 'on 'Change.' But here and there you note one whom you hall-mark 'stockbroker' or 'company director'. Perhaps the 'bus conductor touches his hat to him as he descends at the Mansion House. Possibly the policeman on point duty steps a pace forward as he passes to wish him 'Good morning'. Only a City man can appreciate all that is conveyed by those subtle marks of distinction.

London Bridge! It is the climax, the apotheosis, as it were, of all thus far seen. So crowded is the canvas, so full of movement, it dazes one. Life sweeps over the bridge like the rush of the sea by the sides of a ship – always Citywards. In thousands they advance, leaning forward, with long, quick strides, eager to be there! Swiftly they flash past, and still they come and come, like the silent, shadowy legions of a dream.

Somehow they suggest the dogged march of an army in retreat, with its rallying point far ahead, and the enemy's cavalry pressing on its rear. Looking down upon the swarming masses, with the dark sullen river for a background, they fuse into one monstrous organism, their progress merges in the rhythmic swaying of one mammoth breathing thing. Stand in the midst of the mighty current of men! A wearied, languorous feeling creeps over you, as face follows face, and eyes in thousands swim by. It is the hypnotic influence of the measureless, the unfathomable, the you-know-not-what of mystery and elusiveness in life, stealing your senses away.

During an hour these multitudes in drab march past to the relentless City, to barter what they have of value for their daily bread. The monotony of the endless parade is overpowering, numbing; and minute by minute the railway station, not a stone's throw away, yields up fresh battalions for this sublime muster of citizens. Within the station itself is being enacted a scene which is an impressive combination of order and disorder. A train rushes alongside a platform. In a twinkling its passengers are thronging to the exits. A few seconds more and the place is clear. The empty train disappears to make way for another, whose impatient whistle is already heard. Again a crowd of passengers melts, and another springs up in its place. The train is again shunted, and the metals it vacates are speedily covered. And so proceeds like clockwork the arrangement – so simple and so intricate – for the mobilisation of the army of business men who pour in one wonderful phalanx across the noble bridge.

For a full hour it continues. Then, as the clock points to ten, there are gaps in the ranks. The tide of life suddenly slackens. The reinforcements grow weaker. Traffic once more moves freely in opposite directions; for the invasion of the morning is consummated. Business has begun.

P. F. William Ryan, 1901

THE FATHER OF ALL TRAFFIC JAMS

Over our heads the traffic of the City rolls on, the roar of it coming down to us in the subway at the Bank of England, whither we have travelled by rail, in a bewildering confusion of deep, discordant tones. Let us ascend, choosing for our exit the steps leading to Princes Street. As we mount the steps the noise presses round us, the horses' hoofs ring on the asphalt close by our heads. On the top step we secure a foothold on the eagerly contested pavement space. We set our backs to the wall, and regard a scene which in many respects has no parallel in the wide world.

It is midday, and London's business is at high tide. Those whose working hours commence at eight o'clock, nine o'clock, and ten o'clock have all by this time got into the swing of the day's work. Shoppers and leisurely sightseers add to the throng. At innumerable stages, up to four, five, and six miles away, towards every point of the compass, omnibuses have filled at their conductors' cry, 'Bank! Bank!' Through great stress of traffic have they come, and hither in long, uninterrupted processions do they continue to come. Of all colours are they, and so closely ranged together that they blot out of view all but the upper portions of the buildings. At the will of traffic-managing policemen, now this stream of vehicles, now that, holds the field.

The hubbub of it! Underlying all is the incessant rumble of wheels; but high above that rings the clatter, clatter of hundreds of horses' hoofs on the smooth, hard road. The rustling footsteps of thousands of men and women make a light accompaniment. And this babel of sounds goes on incessantly – a continual hum, and roar, and clatter; till you wonder that the hardest pavement does not wear through in a day, that the toughest human nerve can sustain it for a couple of hours.

Charles Turner, 1903

A CURIOSITY OF WORLD-WIDE INTEREST

Having ascended from the river bank to Cannon or King Street, one has reached the real level of the City, and finds himself in a dense crowd of vehicles and men, which at first produces an altogether bewildering and almost suffocating

An unusually distant view of the famous Royal Exchange traffic jam, taken from the corner of Poultry and Queen Victoria Street. The buses, carts, and cabs seem more orderly than usual, and to be flowing quite freely. The date is after 1905, when the domed no. 1 Cornhill was rebuilt to the designs of the bank specialist J. MacVicar Anderson.

impression; the amount of the traffic here being certainly greater than anywhere else in the world. From the Strand and the Embankment, through Queen Victoria Street, and from Oxford Street and Holborn, through Cheapside, the West rushes its flood of human beings into the City in an uninterrupted line of omnibuses, cabs and carriages. Through Fleet Street 71,677 pedestrians are passing every twelve hours, while the number of those who pass through Cheapside, the most frequented street, within the same time, amounts to 91,190.

Simultaneously three railway lines, the District, Metropolitan and the Electric Tube, carry on below our feet the same work of conveying people from the West to the East. Though long trains are running every three minutes, they are mostly, except those between 12 and 2 o'clock, fully occupied or even overcrowded.

The whole of the traffic is concentrated upon the Bank of England, the Mansion House and the Stock Exchange, whence Cornhill and Lombard Street, Threadneedle and Broad Streets convey the crowds further East, while Moorgate Street and Finsbury Pavement lead further North. In front of the Mansion House, 248,015 pedestrians are passing every day, while 26,200 use the underground passage which was opened here a few years ago. The whole street net of the City is very tortuous and intricate; strange looking alleys and courts, only known to the initiated, lead across the blocks of houses from one street to another. All is crowded by

This 1900 photograph shows the crush before the Mansion House at its classic worst. The view is towards Lombard Street. The Liverpool and London Globe Insurance offices at the corner of Cornhill were rebuilt in 1905, as seen in the photograph on page 88.

business men, clerks and shopmen hurrying along, in winter generally wearing a silk hat, but in summer, often bareheaded. The street scene, say, at the corner of Cheapside, opposite the Bank of England, is certainly a curiosity of world-wide interest.

Carl Peters, 1904

AN EXPENSIVE HABIT

If ever London has her epic poet, I think he will sing the omnibus; but the poet who sings the hansom must be of a lyrical note. I do not see how he could be too lyrical, for anything more like song does not move on wheels, and its rapid rhythm suggests the quick play of fancy in that impetuous form. We have the hansom with us, but it does not perform the essential part in New York life that it does in London life. In New York you *may* take a hansom; in London you *must*. You serve yourself of it as at home you serve yourself of the electric car; but not by any means at the same rate. Nothing is more deceitful than the cheapness of the hansom, for it is of such an immediate and constant convenience that the unwary stranger's shilling has slipped from him in a sovereign before he knows, with the swift succession of occasions when the hansom seems imperative. A 'bus is inexpensive, but it is stolid and bewildering; a hansom is always cheerfully intelligent. It will set you down at the very

place you seek; you need walk neither to it nor from it; a nod, a glance, summons it or dismisses. The 'bus may be kind, but it is not flattering, and the hansom is flattering as well as kind; flattering to one's pride, one's doubt, one's timid hope. It takes all the responsibility for your prompt and unerring arrival; and you may trust it almost implicitly. At any point in London you can bid it go to any other with a confidence that I rarely found abused. Once, indeed, my cabman carried me a long way about at midnight, and when he finally left me at my door, he was disposed to be critical of its remoteness, while he apologized for the delay. I suggested that in a difficulty like his a map of London would be a good thing; but though he was so far in drink as to be able to take the joke in good part, he denied that a map would be of the least use to a cabman. Probably he was right; my map was not of the least use to me; and his craft seemed to feel their way about through the maze of streets and squares and circles by the same instinct that serves a pilot on a river in the dark. Their knowledge is a thing of the nerves, not of the brains, if there is a difference; or if there is none, then it is an affair of the subliminal consciousness, it is inspiration, it is genius. It could not well be overpaid, and the cabmen are careful that it is not underpaid. I heard, indeed, of two American ladies who succeeded in underpaying their cabman; this was their belief resting upon his solemn declaration; but I myself failed in every attempt of the kind. My cabman always said that it was not enough; and then I compromised by giving him too much. Many stories are told of the abusiveness of the class, but a simple and

A hansom cab in 1890. As their numbers grew they had added so much to traffic congestion by cruising for fares that the police required them to wait at a rank between jobs. This cabby's home rank was at Charing Cross station.

effective rule is to overpay them at once and be done with it. I have sometimes had one cast a sorrowing glance at the just fare pressed into his down-stretched palm, and drive off in thankless silence; but any excess of payment was met with eager gratitude. I preferred to buy the cabman's good-will, because I find this is a world in which I am constantly buying the good-will of people whom I do not care the least for, and I did not see why I should make an exception of cabmen. Only once did I hold out against an extortionate demand of theirs. That was with a cabman who drove me to the station, and said: 'I'll have to get another sixpence for this, sir.' 'Well,' I returned, with a hardihood which astonished me, 'you won't get it of me.' But I was then leaving London, and was no longer afraid.

William Dean Howells, 1905

A SKITTISH HORSE

There are not too many hansoms to be met with in the City on a Sunday afternoon; so that you must take what you can get. Otherwise, Horace, who had not a Londoner's comfortable conviction that one horse is much the same as another, would probably have allowed that particular vehicle to pass unhailed.

'Mind his heels!' said he, as Veronica stepped in; and, sure enough, two resounding bangs upon the dashboard gave immediate justification for his warning.

'Is he going to kick?' asked Veronica, while Horace, after calling out the address to the driver, seated himself beside her.

This impression of a hansom cab accident in the Strand illustrated a scene in W.E. Norris's 1894 novel, A Victim of Good Fortune.

'Yes, I expect so,' answered the young man, who looked a little perturbed. 'Shall we let this fellow go and walk on until we meet another?'

But Veronica answered, with a laugh, 'Oh no! That would be too humiliating. Besides, a hansom isn't like a dog-cart. There would be a great deal of kicking to be done before we could be touched.'

That was all very fine, but a hansom is an awkward conveyance to get out of; and they were no sooner off than Horace heartily wished that he had been more peremptory with his companion. The animal was young and fresh; he did not seem to be well accustomed to his work, and what was worse was that the driver was evidently afraid of him. After about five uneasy minutes – during which Veronica had been placidly contemplating the long vista of the Strand – the very thing happened which her more watchful neighbour had been inwardly dreading. A sudden gust of wind swept across the street, blowing a scrap of newspaper before it, just under the horse's nose. Up went the brute's heels, down went his head, and the next moment he was tearing off towards Charing Cross at a pace far too good to last.

It is never very pleasant to be run away with, but perhaps the most disagreeable time and place that could be selected for such an experience would be a London street on Sunday. Horses seldom bolt in a crowd, and even when they do, their career cannot last long; but this excited beast had nothing in front of him, except a couple of omnibuses, with both of which he just missed colliding, and the only question was how far he would run before the inevitable smash occurred.

'Sit tight!' exclaimed Horace. But, indeed, there was nothing else to be done, unless it was to get down into the bottom of the cab, and this measure of precaution he was in the act of enforcing upon Veronica when he was abruptly shot out into the roadway, preceded by his hat, which somebody obligingly picked up for him. The horse had slipped and fallen heavily; the shafts were broken; the driver was lying insensibly upon the pavement, and Veronica, neither frightened nor hurt, was stooping over the man, surrounded by a rapidly increasing crowd. Horace, after satisfying himself that she had really sustained no injury, was for withdrawing her from the throng at once, but to this she could in no wise be induced to consent. Not a step would she stir until a couple of policemen had arrived upon the scene, and the horse had been got upon his legs again, and a stretcher had been procured for the luckless cabman; nor would anything serve her then but to join the procession which was presently set in motion for Charing Cross Hospital.

W. E. Norris, 1894

KNIFE-BOARD AND GARDEN SEAT

The Metropolitan 'bus, as I first knew it, was a very modest vehicle, holding twelve persons inside, and none at all, save the driver, outside. The roof was wholly free from passengers, and years elapsed before there was added to the top of the 'bus two long rows of seats parallel with the sides of the 'bus, and which very soon acquired the popular designation of the 'knife-board'. No females ever climbed to the 'knife-board' eminence; and, indeed, almost the only 'bus with a box seat available for a fair occupant, was the London and Richmond one.

When the London General Omnibus Company – the capital for which was largely subscribed in Paris – began its operations, its promoters held an Exhibition somewhere near Charing Cross, of models of improved omnibuses; and among these I recall several with staircases on the outside, like those attached to the Russian 'isbas', and by means of which the 'knife-board' could be reached. This eventually led to the adoption of what is known as the 'garden-seat' system, and to me it is positively delightful to watch, looking out of window, the transformation of the formerly barren, or at the most, men-folk frequented roofs of the 'buses, into so many brilliant parterres of tastefully dressed ladies, who gaily ascend the staircases, and seat themselves on the commodious benches, at right angles with the longitudinal sides of the 'bus.

I have fallen hopelessly in love with hundreds of brilliant bonnets, and handsome hats, to say nothing of skirts and sunshades of every colour of the rainbow; and I only regret that the altitude of my apartments precluded me from scanning the countenances of the doubtless lovely occupants of the garden-seats. Perhaps, for the sake of domestic peace and quiet, it is better that I should have admired the costumes, and not become acquainted with the fascinating lineaments of the wearers thereof.

George Augustus Sala, 1894

INSIDE

The omnibus, – mere comedy on a bright, dusty, spring or summer day, when its garden-seats shine resplendent in new paint, – becomes rather a thing of grim tragedy on muddy days of winter gloom, when the rain comes down in torrents, and a stern 'Full inside', is all the response the weary wayfarer gets after waiting long minutes, – painful, jostled minutes, – for the desired vehicle.

The omnibus conductors are generally uncommunicative, and often morose – perhaps, from too frequent digs in the ribs from fussy old ladies and choleric old gentlemen. Some of them, too, refuse to wait for you unless you pretend to have a broken leg, or at least to be half-paralyzed; yet, even among 'bus conductors, there are still occasional pearls to be met with. In one thing they show remarkable aptitude; namely, in an interchange of wit with the drivers of rival vehicles. On these occasions their sallies, considering their very limited vocabulary, are often quite brilliantly forcible. In a 'block' in Oxford Street or the Strand, or after a 'liquor-up' at a convenient 'pub', such flights of humour will often while away the time very agreeably for the passenger inside, that is, if he be not too nervously fearful of being drawn into the dispute himself. Omnibus conductors, however, 'frivel' as they may among themselves, are as adamant where any infringement of

A knife-board bus passing through Parliament Square during the 1890s, presumably on its way to Victoria. If so, these City men were going home at a very civilized hour.

their rules by their passengers is concerned. Why they continually insist – against all show of reason too – on seating no less than six fat people on one side of their vehicle, and no more than six thin ones on the other, has always been a mystery to me. It is, however, as a law of the Medes and Persians, for it knows no alteration. But it has at any rate the merit of pointing the parable about the fat and the lean kine.

Fat people, it must be confessed, have a peculiar affinity for omnibuses. The contents of a 'bus are, I have observed, nearly always fat. An omnibus journey is, by the obese, regarded as so much exercise. An old tradesman of my acquaintance who suffered from liver was lately ordered exercise by his doctor. Thereupon he took, like Mrs. Carlyle, one sad shilling's worth of omnibus per day, and was surprised when, at the end of a month, he felt no better. 'One shilling's worth of omnibus!' – horribie suggestion! It must have taken nearly three hours, for the cost of omnibus journeys can generally

be reckoned at a penny for every ten minutes. The distance traversed is immaterial, as the traveller will soon discover. If he wishes to catch any particular train he had better allow twenty minutes a mile to be quite on the safe side.

On rainy days, character in omnibus is yet more self-revealing. Thus, a wayfarer gets in with a wet cloak and wet umbrella; no one shows any desire to make room. The five lean kine on the one side spread themselves out; the five fat ones on the other expand also. The new-comer stumbles, the wet cloak splashes every one, the umbrella drips genially; it is a pleasant sight. When room is finally made and the wanderer seated, the wet garments soon exhale a fragrant steam – which scent mingles with the odours of cabbage, peppermint, or onions, already discernible. These scents, it may be added, vary in different quarters of London. Thus, onions are partial to Long Acre; antiseptics to Southampton Row; cheap scent to Oxford Street and Holborn; whisky, perhaps, to 'the

'Ampstid Road'; general frowsiness to King's Road, Chelsea; and the aroma of elegant furs to the shades of Kensington. Omnibus scents vary, too, with 'the varying year'. In the spring it is leeks and 'spring onions'; in the winter it is paraffin or eucalyptus; in the summer it is indescribable.

Mrs. E. T. Cook, 1902

ON THE BUS

On the 'bus, coming home, thro' streets full of motor traffic and all available space plastered with advertisements that screamed at you, I espied in front three pretty girls, who gave me the 'Glad Eye'. One had a deep, musical voice, and kept on using it, one of the others a pretty ankle and kept on showing it.

At Kew, two Italians came aboard, one of whom went out of his way to sit among the girls. He sat level with them, and kept turning his head around, giving them a sweeping glance as he did so, to shout remarks in Italian to his friend behind. He thought the girls were prostitutes, I think, and he may have been right. I was on the seat behind this man and for want of anything better to do, studied his face minutely. In short, it was

fat, round, and greasy. He wore black moustachios with curly ends, his eyes were dark, shining, bulgy, and around his neck was wrapped a scarf inside a dirty linen collar, as if he had a sore throat. I sat behind him and hated him steadily, perseveringly.

At Hammersmith the three girls got off, and the bulgy-eyed Italian watched them go with lascivious eyes, looking over the rail and down at them on the pavement – still interested. I looked down too. They crossed the road in front of us and disappeared.

'W. N. P. Barbellion', 1914

BEAUTY v. UTILITY

Since 1906 the tram-cars of the London County Council have run along the Embankment. The fight for powers to bring the cars across the bridges began as far back as 1870. Bill after bill, promoted first by private companies, and then by the London County Council, was rejected on the plea that the Embankment would be spoilt, but at last, in 1906, Parliament acquiesced, and before the end of that year the cars from Westminster Bridge were running to within a few

Driver (approaching Hyde Park Corner and pointing out the sights to country visitors). "On the left's the statue erected to the memory of the Great Dook o' Wellington, and that 'ere on the right's a statue erected to the memory of the pore ole 'oss-'buses wot's been run orf the street by them stinkin' motors."

The first motor bus was licensed in 1897. Fifteen years later there were few horse buses left, and it was time for a comic elegy.

THE GREAT TRAM v. MOTOR-BUS QUESTION.
The Motor-bus (triumphantly). "THERE YOU ARE, LOOK AT ME! I DON'T HAVE TO RUN IN A SILLY OLD GROOVE. I CAN GO WHERE I LIKE."

No sooner had the motor bus driven the poor old horse bus from the road, than it was in the thick of a new struggle with the electric tram. This was Punch's *comment in 1912, on the main plank of the pro-bus argument, mobility.*

The London County Council had a long struggle to get trams on to the Embankment, but eventually managed it in 1908, as part of the Kingsway scheme. The special single-decker trams ran through a tunnel from beside Waterloo Bridge to the northern end of Kingsway, where one is here seen emerging c. 1910. Between 1929 and 1931 the tunnel was deepened to take double-deckers.

yards of the eastern end of the Embankment at Blackfriars Bridge. In April, 1908, the northern and southern lines were linked up by the opening of an underground tramway from the Embankment to Aldwych. The last step in the process will be the bringing of the cars over Blackfriars Bridge, which is now (1909) being widened with that end in view. A circular service will then be practicable: the cars, instead of having to be reversed at the eastern end of the Embankment, will be able to continue their course over Blackfriars Bridge and so round to Westminster Bridge.

W. W. Hutchings, 1909

A NEW PLEASURE . . .

The cult of the motor-car has had a belated growth in London. The writers who foresaw that, apart from utilitarian reasons, steam or electric traction on the King's highway was a potential amusement were for a time as voices crying vainly in the wilderness. But London has become converted, and

even in Hyde Park the drivers of the automobiles speed merrily on the macadam road which skirts the Row that is sacred to equestrians. Many ladies drive their own machines, whether these latter be of English, French, or American make.

As an amusement 'motoring' is incomparable; the mechanism nowadays is so exact that complete control is almost absolutely assured to the driver.

Gilbert Burgess, 1903

To see Motoring London at its best, one must take one's stand on certain of the great traffic conduits leading outwards from the metropolis, when on high days, holidays, and at week ends, all Londoners who possess engines and gear over four wheels, whirl and skir, trumpet and hoot, country-wards and seawards to escape the city for a little space. It is then, and only then, when every minute sees the passage of a car bearing its freight of cloaked and head-shrouded women and heavily coated and goggled men to pure air and open heath, along the pleasant roads of the home counties, that the wholesale manner in which motoring has popularised itself can be fully realised. From the spitting, fast-flitting motor-bicycle, with its rigid rider, up through the gamut of motor-tricycle – carrying a single passenger or hauling a light trailer with family loads – motor-quad, voiturette, light car and heavily engined automobile, roofed and hooded and screened, all sorts and conditions of the self-propelled proffer themselves in an incredibly short space of time. Motoring London makes then all haste it can to get out of London and leave the town behind it. Vehicles worth thousands of pounds surge by in one short hour, and from morn to dewy eve and late into the night the dwellers along suburban roads are never free of the roar of the passing cars. By good fortune the observer may even be able to catch sight of the King in one of his roomy cars hastening down to Windsor.

H. O. Tyman, 1903

. . . AND A NEW PAIN

London is, if anything, rather more infested than New York with motors, as the English more simply and briefly call automobiles. The perspective is seldom free of them, and from time to time the air is tainted with their breath, which is now one of the most characteristic stenches of civilization. They share equally with other vehicles the drives in the parks, though their speed is tempered there to the prevalent pace. They add to the general noise the shuddering bursts of their swift percussions, and make the soul shrink from a forecast of what the aeroplane may be when it shall come hurtling overhead with some peculiar screech as yet unimagined.

William Dean Howells, 1905

A busy scene outside the automobile engineering works of Tomlinson and Kersey at 2 Great Central Street, by Marylebone station, c. 1910.

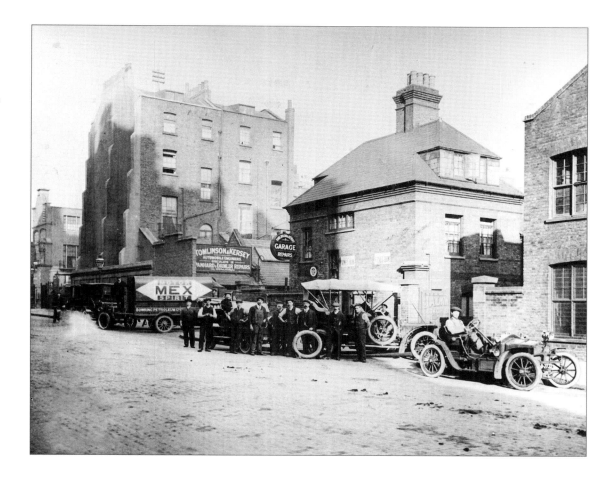

FIRST AND THIRD

On one occasion when I travelled down from Charing Cross by a train that was crammed, a friendly guard managed to reserve me a carriage, and, just as we were steaming out of the terminus, remarked:

'You will be all right in here, Mr. Montagu. There will be nobody to disturb you. I think I can guarantee that you will have the carriage to yourself all the way.'

'L'homme propose,' etc. We did not call at Cannon Street, whence another section of the train started, but we did stop at London Bridge. On the platform were, among others, a man and woman, and five children, with a perambulator and sundry articles of luggage of many forms and sizes. The man ran one way, the woman the other, and the porters hurried hither and thither; but seats could nowhere be found in the train. Husband and wife met in the immediate neighbourhood of my carriage, and cried in accents of despair and excitement:

'There is no room! There is no room anywhere!'

'You must wait for the next train,' said the guard; and I shall never forget the look of disappointment this remark conjured up upon the faces of the five children, who ranged from a girl of about fourteen to a great chubby boy of three.

I was extremely ill at the time, but this sight was more than I could stand, so, calling out of the window to the guard, who was about to give the signal for the train to start, I bade him unlock the door of my compartment and bundle the family in. Father, perambulator, mother, parcels, children – in

they came pell-mell; the whistle was blown, and we were in motion, as well as commotion.

On looking round I discovered that my invitation had been more widely accepted than I had contemplated. Taking advantage of the state of affairs, a couple of late arrivals in the persons of a coster and a young woman had scrambled into the carriage. Thus we were a party of ten. It was a sultry July afternoon, and the outlook was anything but pleasant. However, things soon settled down.

The father of the family sat opposite me at one end of the carriage, his wife and children took up positions in the centre, and the uninvited pair occupied the remaining window seats. It transpired during the journey that the coster and the young woman had been married that morning, and were on their way to spend a three days' honeymoon at Ramsgate. Their luggage consisted of a small hand-bag, containing, I presume, a brush and comb, a pair of irons for the lady's handsome fringe, and other articles of the toilet.

'Now then, Ikey,' said my opposite neighbour as we steamed through Spa Road, 'leave that thar bird alone. He'll get shaking enough without your rolling him about.'

Looking round, I perceived, in the centre of the carriage, and on the top of a pile of packages, a small cage in which was a linnet. Hard by, I noticed a rush basket, which also, as was proved by its oscillating movement, contained live-stock of some description or other. My curiosity being aroused, I ventured to ask what the basket contained.

'Oh, 'im?' my *vis-à-vis* remarked, jerking his thumb in the direction of the receptacle in question, ''e's the cat – Joe, as

we calls 'im. Rachel, if you've got a knife in your pocket, cut one of the strings and give poor Joe some air, for 'e didn't get much from 'Oxton to London Bridge; or perhaps, sir, if you and these 'ere gentleman and lady' – meaning the coster and his bride – 'haven't no objection, Joe might come out for a bit and stretch himself.'

The happy pair at once gave their consent, and I, for my part, did not object to the proposal, though I ventured to suggest that the linnet might.

'Lor' bless yer, sir,' said the man, with a smile, 'they don't mind one another. We are, thank God, a happy and united family, and the cat knows it's the children's bird, and would no more think o' touching it than of jumping out of this 'ere window. Joe's used to railways, sir. We come this journey every year, there and back, and Joe knows when the time comes, and enjoys it just as much as Becky, my eldest girl, or any of the young 'uns.'

Joe had now emerged from captivity, and was alternately playing with the children and rubbing his chin against the bars of the linnet's cage.

Montagu Williams, 1892

EXCURSIONISTS

We find the holiday note dominant when we push our way through the seething crowd that fills Liverpool Street on a summer Saturday afternoon. Everywhere we come upon young people laughing and joking together. The young ladies

are in their Sunday best, the young gentlemen have their hats rakishly set and display considerable daring in the colour of their neckties. Some are on cricket bent, others are anglers; there are tennis players, in fact, nearly every branch of outdoor sport is represented on the platform. Then there are the hard-working boys and girls out for a mere holiday trip, and you can see that they mean to make the most of every minute. The moment they have stormed the train and packed themselves in their places, the sound of the concertina is heard, and the popular song rings out loud and clear under the glass roof. They will sing till they reach their destination. If they return at night, they will sing all the way back. At midnight, as they make their way tired and sleepy out of the station into the silent streets of the City, they will still march to the uplifting strains of the concertina or the mouth-organ and sing. Sometimes they will dance, but that depends largely on the length of the journey and the atmospheric conditions.

George R. Sims, 1901

NOTES FROM THE UNDERGROUND

By the courtesy of Mr. Powell, manager of the District Railway, I was provided with an 'engine-pass' for the 'Inner Circle'; and on a bright June morning I made my way to St. James's Park station. There I met Chief-Inspector Exall, who was detailed to accompany and look after me generally.

In a short time our train rushed into the station, and a moment later we had boarded the engine. I was

Liverpool Street, London's busiest terminus, as it appeared c. 1905. The station, designed by Edward Wilson, was opened in 1874, and extended in 1891. Its grand façade and chaotic interior are now only memories.

accommodated with a position near the left-hand tank, whence I could get an uninterrupted view ahead; but it had its drawbacks as the water in that tank was hot.

No time is wasted at stations on the Underground, and a minute later the train was off – off into a black wall ahead with the shrieking of ten thousand demons rising above the thunder of the wheels. The sensation altogether was much like the inhalation of gas preparatory to having a tooth drawn. I would have given a good deal to have waited just a minute or so longer. Visions of accidents, collisions, and crumbling tunnels floated through my mind; a fierce wind took away my breath, and innumerable blacks filled my eyes. I crouched low and held on like grim death to a little rail near me. Driver, stoker, inspector, and engine – all had vanished. Before and behind and on either side was blackness, heavy, dense and impenetrable. Westminster Bridge, Charing Cross, and the Temple were passed before I could do or think of anything beyond holding on to that rolling, rushing engine: then finding that I was still alive and sound, I began

to look about me. Inspector Exall put his head to my ear and shouted something at the top of his voice, but I could only catch the word 'Blackfriars.' I looked ahead. Far off in the distance was a small square-shaped hole, seemingly high up in the air, and from it came four silver threads palpitating like gossamers in the morning breeze. Larger and larger grew the hole, the threads became rails, and the hole a station; Blackfriars, with rays of golden sunlight piercing through the gloom.

Frederick T. Jane, 1893

We took the underground for returning to Wimbledon. Our train was full of the City men whom I have surnamed 'Baggies', because, instead of the leather portfolio which Frenchmen carry, these men always have a leather bag. I was struck, as I always am, by the expression of utter weariness on their faces.

THE UNDERGROUND RAILWAY – AS IT SHOULD BE.
GUARD (*to choking and coughing female*): *"Here, take a Géraudel's Pastille, and welcome! The Company provides 'em. I've never been afraid of damp, fog, or cold since I carried a case of Géraudels."*

The foul atmosphere of the old Underground was a boon to the enterprising advertiser, as in this 1896 recommendation of a throat pastille.

Some of them looked as though they could scarcely turn the pages of their newspapers. Their Parisian confrères never have that worn-out appearance. In their day, which is relatively short, these Englishmen have to get through an enormous amount of work and, consequently, the strain is very great both for mind and body. As I watched them I could not help anticipating their precious week-end, which ensures them at least thirty-six hours of rest and peace.

I always admire the way in which Englishmen get in and out of a train. There is never any awkwardness or hurry. It seems to me always that their movements are regulated more mathematically than ours.

On all the platforms of the underground, there are women and girls to be seen wearing very light-coloured dresses, frequently white ones, feather boas and picture hats. They ride on the tops of the omnibuses in the same style of dress. The English women have no sense of the harmony of things.

The walls of the underground are of course covered with advertisements. Such posters are neither as pretty nor as artistic as ours, but they are more ingenious and more startling. They make a brutal impression on the brain. After a week spent in England, one comes away with a whole collection of these. I have *Scrubbs' Ammonia* and *Sunlight Soap* fixed permanently behind my forehead. A few years ago, the great blot on the poster of *Stephens' Ink* caught my eye. I bought a bottle of it and since then I have always used it. This is certainly a good instance of suggestion. All these commonplace advertisements, absurd as they sometimes are, have their purpose. They have to produce a little effect of some kind, they help life.

Augustine Favre de Coulevain, 1906–11

The weather was for the most part divinely beautiful, so tenderly and evenly cool and warm, with a sort of lingering fondness in the sunshine, as if it were prescient of the fogs so soon to blot it. The first of these came on the last day of our research, when suddenly we dropped from the clouded surfaces of the earth to depths where the tube-line trains carry their passengers from one brilliantly lighted station to another. We took three of the different lines, experimentally, rather than necessarily, in going from St. Mary Woolnoth, in Lombard Street, hard by the Bank of England, to the far neighborhood of Stoke Newington; and at each descent by the company's lift, we left the dark above ground, and found the light fifty feet below. While this sort of transit is novel, it is delightful; the air is good, or seems so, and there is a faint earthy smell, somewhat like that of stale incense in Italian churches, which I found agreeable from association at least; besides, I liked to think of passing so far beneath all the superincumbent death and all the superambulant life of the immense immemorial town.

William Dean Howells, 1905

Chapter 9

POVERTY AND CHARITY

Slumming was one of the Society fads of the 1880s. At its most frivolous it involved duchesses being driven up and down the Whitechapel Road and exclaiming afterwards, 'Do you call that a slum? Why, it's one of the finest streets in London. I don't believe in all this fuss about the housing of the poor.' The other extreme is found in the dedicated work of the missions, 'like late revivals of the monastic system of the middle ages', where university men took up temporary residence to learn and to teach. Toynbee Hall in Whitechapel was the first of these. Oxford House at Bethnal Green was the best known of several that followed. Sometimes the process was reversed and working men were invited to Oxford or Cambridge. There is a story of an undergraduate entertaining some of these unfamiliar guests in his rooms. 'He had not been to the terrible East End, but he had been told to talk "quite naturally, as you would to men of your own class". At first he was a little shy, but he at last ventured on the following remark to his neighbour: "Ahem! many people in town just now?" The workman looked at him with a withering, pitiful gaze, and said, somewhat bluntly, "About five millions".'

Toynbee Hall offended some by its careful avoidance of religious teaching. In response to this imagined threat most of the churches made somewhat similar efforts, in which they were careful to remedy the omission. The East End was the fashionable scene of such enterprises, much to the disgust of many in the scarcely less impoverished south, and at times Whitechapel and Bethnal Green were awash with competing missionaries and social workers, all eager to press their assistance upon the deserving poor. As Charles Booth said of the immensely diverse activities of one Spitalfields mission, 'excepting independence almost every virtue is inculcated'.

The danger was that the motive behind the charitable efforts of the West End and the universities would cease to be humanity or conscience and become curiosity or the quest for sensational research material. The zoo in one direction and the East End in another had a similar educational function for some young intellectuals like Barbellion's friend 'R.' 'Not infrequently he visits the East End to study "how the poor live", he lectures at Toynbee Hall, and calls the proletariat "the prolly".'

Providence Place was a network of alleyways on the south-west side of Middlesex Street (Petticoat Lane), in the heart of the Jewish quarter. The photograph was taken in 1909.

FULL FEATHER

No one who is a stranger to the East End of London can have any idea of the kind of female headgear in vogue in that locality. The material is cotton velvet, the colour, gaudy, and the size, enormous; and let me parenthetically observe that, no matter how shabby or dirty be the rest of the clothing of the ladies to be seen in every street, court, and alley in the neighbourhood of Commercial Road, Whitechapel, and Shoreditch, if they have any covering at all to their heads, it is certain to be one of the hats to which I refer. In a case that came before me some time ago it transpired that these head ornaments are, in many instances, let out on hire, at so much per week or month; and I have frequently had testimony borne to the fact that the East End girls will part with everything they possess in the world – will sell themselves, body and soul – to become the proud possessors of the articles in question. The size and colour of the feathers are points on which there is keen rivalry among the denizens of court and alley. Day by day, at the Thames and Worship Street Police Courts, the women of the locality are brought before the sitting magistrate, on charges of drunkenness, assault, and so forth; and though their dresses may be torn and blood-stained, and their faces scratched and otherwise disfigured, there, sure enough, is the accustomed hat, cocked jauntily on one side, and having apparently escaped all injury. Whether these Amazons are careful to bare their heads before coming to close quarters, I am unable to say.

Montagu Williams, 1892

'AMMERSMITH
"What sort of a stone do yer call that as yer've got in yer ring, 'Arriet?"
"Well! dunno: but my chap says as 'e thinks as it's a 'Ammersmith."

The costermonger's girl and her hat as seen by Phil May in 1893.

In the gutter. A suitably Bohemian looking sandwich-board man outside the National Gallery during the winter of 1913.

THE LAST RUNG

I know of no more wearisome occupation than that of the sandwich man. In fair weather and foul, in sunshine and snow, in clouds of dust and storms of rain, he has to jog along throughout the dreary day, attracting public notice to the strong woman at the Aquarium, the performing elephants at the Crystal Palace, or the latest Ceylon blend at the sign of the Golden Cannister.

From time to time the boardsman has to don some descriptive costume. Should he be retained on behalf of the Army and Navy Hair-Cutting Saloon, he may appear in an old regimental tunic and cocked hat, accompanied by a mate who stalks the world in the guise of a British Admiral. Again, should his boards illustrate 'The Convict's Doom', the latest melodramatic success at the Princess's Theatre, he will very likely walk abroad in knickerbockers and a jacket plentifully embellished with the broad arrow.

The remuneration of sandwich men varies from one

shilling to one and eightpence per day. To earn this paltry amount the poor fellows have to tramp through the streets from ten in the morning to ten at night. Once during the day a halt is called for a meal, or, if that is not forthcoming, for a pipe.

In spite of the badness of the pay, the long hours, and the degradation involved, there is keen competition for the sandwich boards. The regular hands, who are known to the advertising contractors, are tolerably sure of obtaining employment, but the case is very different with the occasional men. Of such there are often fifty to every board that has to be carried. I know of no more striking illustration of the struggle for existence than is afforded by the exterior of the contractors' offices when men are being engaged. It is painful to see the eager and anxious faces of the applicants during the distribution of boards, and still more painful afterwards to see the unsuccessful ones filing dejectedly away, some to seek work elsewhere, and others to betake themselves to the parks, the day nurseries of poor wretches who have not had the means, on the previous evening, to procure a night's lodging in a 'doss-house'.

The sandwich men are drawn from nearly every class and calling. Almost any one can carry boards; hence the desperate fight for the work.

Few men sink any lower than this employment, for the simple reason that they do not long survive it. For the most part they end their days in the workhouse infirmary or the hospital, whither they are taken when stricken by ague or other disease induced by exposure to the cold and wet.

Montagu Williams, 1892

The graceful dancing of slum children sounds like a sentimental fable, but it has been recorded by too many writers and artists, some of them grimly realistic, to be disbelieved. This scene was sketched by Dorothy Tennent in 1886.

LIFE ROMPING IN THE BLOOD

There is one beautiful sight in the East End, and only one, and it is the children dancing in the street when the organ-grinder goes his round. It is fascinating to watch them, the new-born, the next generation, swaying and stepping, with pretty little mimicries and graceful inventions all their own, with muscles that move swiftly and easily, and bodies that leap airily, weaving rhythms never taught in dancing school.

I have talked with these children, here, there, and everywhere, and they struck me as being bright as other children, and in many ways even brighter. They have most active little imaginations. Their capacity for projecting themselves into the realm of romance and fantasy is remarkable. A joyous life is romping in their blood. They delight in music, and motion, and colour, and very often they betray a startling beauty of face and form under their filth and rags.

But there is a Pied Piper of London Town who steals them all away. They disappear. One never sees them again, or anything that suggests them. You may look for them in vain amongst the generation of grown-ups. Here you will find stunted forms, ugly faces, and blunt and stolid minds. Grace, beauty, imagination, all the resiliency of mind and muscle, are

gone. Sometimes, however, you may see a woman, not necessarily old, but twisted and deformed out of all womanhood, bloated and drunken, lift her draggled skirts and execute a few grotesque and lumbering steps upon the pavement. It is a hint that she was once one of those children who danced to the organ-grinder. Those grotesque and lumbering steps are all that is left of the promise of childhood. In the befogged recesses of her brain has arisen a fleeting memory that she was once a girl. The crowd closes in. Little girls are dancing beside her, about her, with all the pretty graces she dimly recollects, but can no more than parody with her body. Then she pants for breath, exhausted, and stumbles out through the circle. But the little girls dance on.

The children of the Ghetto possess all the qualities which make for noble manhood and womanhood; but the Ghetto itself, like an infuriated tigress turning on its young, turns upon and destroys all these qualities, blots out the light and laughter, and moulds those it does not kill into sodden and forlorn creatures, uncouth, degraded, and wretched below the beasts of the field.

Jack London, 1903

TAMING

He has appeared before the 'beak' as an incorrigible truant of about ten weeks' standing. In some cases, we are sorry to state, he has committed some petty theft, and the magistrate very properly sends him to Upton House or Highbury Grove instead of the jail. At school he works as a half-timer – that is to say, half his day is given to learning, and the other half to industrial occupations. When he is considered sufficiently regenerated he receives a 'license' to return home, on the distinct understanding that he shall regularly attend an efficient day-school. It sometimes happens, we grieve to add, that John relapses into Johnny. Of about a thousand licenses at Highbury Grove, twenty-five per cent have been revoked, and the truants have resumed the discipline of correction; but so successful is the system in the main that when he leaves this or the kindred school John distinguishes himself by making ninety per cent of possible attendances at a day-school – a proportion which puts to the blush the virtuous youngsters throughout London who never play truant. Indeed, the course of training at Highbury and Upton House excites a suspicion that for Johnny to be remitted by the magistrate to the care of Mr. Walker or Mr. Peal is a blessing which makes his truancy an unconscious pursuit of evil that good may come. In the tailor's shop John is a perfect prodigy in turning out trousers, vests, and jackets. The manual training in woodwork gives him a taste which may develop hereafter into voluntary attendance at evening technical schools. More than that, he is sometimes taught to bake the bread for the school, and so gets an excellent education as a baker. Of his proficiency in the usual elementary subjects there are gratifying reports from Her

Majesty's Inspectors. The utmost care is taken of his religious instruction, and his health defies epidemics. In a word, John (despite the occasional relapse into Johnny) is one of the most striking proofs of that solid progress in education from which public attention is too often distracted by unprofitable controversy about the London School Board.

Of course, there is always some dissatisfied person who cannot be convinced even when the efficacy of a system stares him in the face. So inveterate is the prejudice in some minds against compulsory education that even this corrective of truancy is likely to be held up to odium as a piece of tyranny. 'And why should boys be snatched from their parents in this manner?' we can hear the dissatisfied one complain. 'What is to compensate a mother for the loss of her child? Why should the delight of her eyes be taken from her and shut up in a penitentiary, where she cannot visit him?' Here we may quote the school regulation which says: 'Parents are allowed to visit their children once a month on condition of good behaviour.' 'Whose good behaviour?' demands the dissatisfied one. 'Is a mother to be torn from the embraces of her child if she makes a painful exhibition of her maternal emotions, and even inveighs against the despotism which keeps him from his home and his natural guardians?' Possibly this sentimental captiousness will be intensified by another regulation: 'Parents contribute a small amount per week towards the maintenance of the child while under detention, the sum being fixed by the magistrate and collected by the Home Office.' So, while John is shut up in what his mother considers a jail, an oppressive Government forces her to pay something towards the expense of keeping him. This view of State education is not such a burlesque as it may seem, for much that is equally unreasonable

The dark side of the London School Board's work was seen in its draconian truant schools, the two residential institutions at Highbury and Hackney (one of which is shown here) and the day school in Drury Lane.

has been seriously put forward by people who hold that parental rights ought always to be paramount. On that point the words of Mr. Walker have an instructive bearing: 'When we think of the wretched houses and miserable surroundings of many of the boys, the dreadful destitution which exists, the evil influences and bad examples which are so common to them, the entire absence of anything approaching proper control, it is surprising that such good results have been achieved.' It would be impossible to put more forcibly and impressively the difficulties with which the London School Board has to deal, and which illustrate a social problem beyond the ken of persons who fancy that young London would grow up to their entire satisfaction if it were only left alone.

Illustrated London News, 1893

HELL IS A CITY MUCH LIKE LONDON

The Yiddish colony is also a city by itself. The Jews who foregather in Whitechapel are mostly of Polish, Russian, or German extraction, and their talk, to unused ears, sounds like a strange German lingo, unpleasantly whined through the nose. Indeed, it closely resembles German; the word 'Yiddish' itself being but a corruption of the German 'Yüdisch', or Jewish. These people, whose 'interpreters' figure largely at nearly every police-court brawl in Whitechapel, Shoreditch, and Spitalfields, may be said to be a law and dispensation to themselves. They crowd, in their numbers, into dirty tenement houses, in yet dirtier streets; streets in which they barter, buy and sell with all the instinct and all the indomitable energy of their race. Here are the tailors' sweating dens, so often deplored by philanthropic 'commissions'; here human toil is reduced, for the benefit of the 'middleman', to its lowest possible price. The so-called 'Jewish slave-market', to the existence of which attention has been called in the Press, is a strange and unpleasing custom. Here the Jewish 'slave-owner' is, more or less, in the place of the Italian 'padrone', in that he imports human material, and 'farms out' human labour:

Only recently Lord Rothschild described it as a 'new Poland,' and said that it was the business of the nation 'first to humanise it and then Anglicise it.' It certainly wants humanising.

The cosmopolitanism of London tends to draw to it the sweepings, as well as the choice spirits, – the worst, as well as the best, – of all other nations and climes. 'Hell is a city much like London,' said the poet Shelley; and he spoke truth. Views, religious and otherwise, differ largely as to what Hell may be; one opinion, however, may be safely hazarded; that it will at any rate be cosmopolitan.

Mrs. E. T. Cook, 1902

THE RISING FLOOD

The whole district has been affected by the increase of the Jewish population. It has been like the slow rising of a flood. Street after street is occupied. Family follows family. No Gentile could live in

The female staff of the Jews' Free School, Middlesex Street (otherwise known as Petticoat Lane), in 1908.

the same house with these poor foreign Jews, and even as neighbours they are unpleasant; and, since people of this race, though sometimes quarrelsome amongst themselves, are extremely gregarious and sociable, each small street or group of houses invaded tends to become entirely Jewish. Houses are bought or rented, however dilapidated they may be, or with however short a lease to run. The previous tenants are ejected, nominally for repairs, and their place is taken by the new owners or their new tenants, the houses being let and sublet and packed full of poor Jews. The crowding that results is very great, and the dirt reported as indescribable. House and land values rise, however. Rents are punctually paid by the tenants in chief, and are without doubt no less punctually collected from their sub-tenants.

Jewish influence is everywhere discernible. Chapels are superseded by synagogues, parish churches are left stranded; Jewish children are being largely enrolled even in the Church schools, and an increasing number of the Board schools are being obliged to adopt Jewish holidays. The Jews have their local representatives in Parliament and on the Borough Council; the self-managed working men's clubs are in their hands; at one time they nearly monopolised the People's Palace; and in Spitalfields they have taken possession of a benevolent society, a special object of which, earlier in the century, was to give help to the descendants of Protestant Huguenots!

Charles Booth, 1902

HUNGER

I walked up Mile End Road between the Carter and the Carpenter. Mile End Road is a wide thoroughfare, cutting the heart of East London, and there were tens of thousands of people abroad on it. I tell you this so that you may fully appreciate what I shall describe in the next paragraph. As I say, we walked along, and when they grew bitter and cursed the land, I cursed with them, cursed as an American waif would curse, stranded in a strange and terrible land. And, as I tried to lead them to believe, and succeeded in making them believe, they took me for a 'seafaring man', who had spent his money in riotous living, lost his clothes (no unusual occurrence with seafaring men ashore), and was temporarily broke while looking for a ship. This accounted for my ignorance of English ways in general and casual wards in particular, and my curiosity concerning the same.

The Carter was hard put to keep the pace at which we walked (he told me that he had eaten nothing that day), but the Carpenter, lean and hungry, his grey and ragged overcoat flapping mournfully in the breeze, swung on in a long and tireless stride which reminded me strongly of the plains wolf or coyote. Both kept their eyes upon the pavement as they walked and talked, and every now and then one or the other would stoop and pick something up, never missing the stride the while. I thought it was cigar and cigarette stumps they were collecting, and for some time took no notice. Then I did notice.

From the slimy, spittle-drenched sidewalk, they were picking up bits of orange peel, apple skin, and grape stems, and they were eating them. The pits of greengage plums they cracked between their teeth for the kernels inside. They picked up stray crumbs of bread the size of peas, apple cores so black and dirty one would not take them to be apple cores, and these things these two men took into their mouths, and chewed them, and swallowed them; and this, between six and seven o'clock in the evening of August 20, year of our Lord 1902, in the heart of the greatest, wealthiest, and most powerful empire the world has ever seen.

Jack London, 1903

Frederick Charrington, the temperance campaigner (and brewing heir), organised regular Sunday afternoon services and distributions of food, like the one seen here c. 1907, at the Great Assembly Hall in the Mile End Road.

THE LATIN QUARTER

No part of the world presents in such a small area so many singular and interesting pictures of cosmopolitan life as Soho, which is the cherished home of foreign artists, dancers, musicians, singers, and other talented performers, and the sanctuary of political refugees, conspirators, deserters, and defaulters of all nations.

To the initiated Soho is a land of romance – a Bohemia and an Alsatia. But to the British country cousin it is mainly a conglomeration of odd characters. He may imagine himself in the Quartier Latin, or in Santa Lucia, or within the boundaries of a far-off ghetto; he finds himself in a crowd of men, women, and children of alien types – hatchet-faced Greeks, strong-featured Jews, sallow Frenchmen, yellow-skinned Levantines, Swiss and Italians, fair and dark, turbaned Moors, fezzed Kabiles, and ebony sons of Africa. To behold these people on their arrival in the little hotels of Soho is both interesting and instructive. Many of them have undergone sea voyages, as the labels of their luggage denote; and they reveal themselves in the curious garbs of their native countries. In a day or two they will, with few exceptions, be all dressed in the clothes of modern civilisation. The red and white turbans and the fez of the Turks, the yellow koofieh of the Syrians, the conic headgear of the Persians, the toques of the Montenegrins, the fur caps of the Russians and the Poles, will disappear, and so will the stately kaftans, the picturesque baggy trousers, the embroidered vests, the ample kilts, and the greasy sheep-skins. They will all be relegated to the bottom of old-fashioned hair-covered trunks.

Everywhere in Soho there are queer announcements of foreign wares and eatables. Wine shops, too, are numerous, and at night attract small groups of foreigners who indulge in heated discussion.

All these people eat and drink in restaurants according to their means. In them one may breakfast and dine at almost any price; one may partake of the *cuisine bourgeoise*, which allows a variety of dishes, in addition to two vegetables, a dessert, a *petit café* and *pain à discretion* for eightpence: or if one prefers the *cucine alla casa lingua*, which includes a *minestra*, a *regaglia di pollo*, a piece of Gorgonzola, a glass of Italian wine, and a large piece of bread, the expense will be the same.

In the German houses, which also cater for Swedes, Danes, and Norwegians, the *Mittags Essen* (midday meal) costs as little as fourpence. It is simple and filling, but then these Northerns are thirsty souls, and spend in *Lager Bier* what they economise in other ways.

There are restaurants where one may dine at eighteenpence, wine included, and others again where the table d'hôte costs three or five shillings. Many of them send dinners and suppers out at any hour, even in the middle of the night if required. Again, there are not a few that have hardly any customers in the daytime, but in which at night men and women pass through the dining-room upstairs, and through a side door. You hear laughter, and sometimes shrieks and sounds of quarrelling. Soon after all the lights disappear, and all is silent. Someone watching from an upper window has seen the police. This is one of the commonest phases of Soho life.

Count E. Armfelt, 1901

Cosmopolitan Soho in 1914. Wedde's hotel and restaurant occupied 12 and 13a Greek Street.

A political meeting in Trafalgar Square, c. 1901. The crowd contains one lady's bonnet, one turban, and one top hat, property of a journalist. In the background is the pleasantly restrained façade of Morley's Hotel.

A LION IN TRAFALGAR SQUARE

It was a detachment of the Army of the Workless, which was to concentrate this afternoon upon Trafalgar Square. And so, being interested, and desirous for one's own satisfaction of comparing the unemployed of London with their brethren of Sydney and Melbourne, one took heavy overcoat, and woollen comforter, and thick gloves – for it was bitterly cold outside where the hungry manoeuvred without any of these necessaries – and went by devious byways towards the foot of Nelson's column.

One walked about through the meeting, ever conscious that warm clothing, and having recently been fed, were good reasons for personal unpopularity. And so one was not surprised at being curtly requested to 'Go to hell,' when one attempted to open up a conversation with a thin man who coughed strenuously at intervals and spat always. It was obvious that the proper place for a thick overcoat and a comforter and gloves was outside the crowd. Therefore one prowled about the sad outskirts and listened to the speeches of the orators – who, at any rate, and with one exception, did not look as if they suffered from starvation.

There was a red banner on the platform, on which was inscribed in white letters the legend, 'The Freedom of the Working Classes is Slavery or Starvation,' but contemplation of it did not excite the crowd. The crowd was too genuinely empty to become excited about anything. It must have been a woefully uninteresting audience to harangue. It was miserably unresponsive.

Towards the end, however, there rose up a thin, unhealthy, miserable man – with yet a fierce vitality in his bearing, and just that desperate, wrathful eye that catches you and holds you, –

who seemed to stir them a little. He was frankly revolutionary. His logic was avowedly the logic of the tightened waist-belt – unambiguous and direct, and quite without compromise. There was something in the man, showing clearly enough that he meant what he said. Obviously, he was not seeking a seat on the London County Council, or a passage into Parliament. It was hunger that loosened his tongue.

Sometimes his voice cracked and broke; sometimes he stopped to cough. Always the wind fluttered his rags. He was a strange, terrible, uncouth figure, as one silhouetted him from below against the eddying wreaths of mist that made his background. Truly, he was a man of wrath – hungry, reckless wrath, – a veritable *sans culotte*. Now and then he screamed at his audience; often he shook his fist at the National Gallery, or waved his claw-like open hand at the drifting greyness overhead; sometimes he spat fiercely, one almost fancied, into the white, upturned faces at his feet. And intermittently he coughed as if his words were choking him.

But he stirred that tired crowd. The Prime Minister, he shrieked, was the most callous Prime Minister that England had ever known. If his hearers had half the pluck and energy of the men of former days they would do deeds which would strike terror into the hearts of their rulers. Let them go where the wealth was made, and make the wealthy uncomfortable by their presence. To achieve anything they would have to put the fears of the masses into the hearts of the classes. They should make the latter see that they (the masses) were not only prepared to make violent speeches, but to carry out their threats. And so forth.

This is a mild version of what he said – a very mild and second-hand version. The burden of it all was that the East should raid the West. It was a wild, half-mad speech, – but it caught on. It took that weary, hungry concourse by the shoulders and shook it. It appealed to its temper, it moved it. Low, sullen, growling responses drifted up to the eager speaker. A hum of approval greeted each savage period, gasped out in fierce earnestness.

But it was only lip-fervour that they gave him back. When he screeched for men to follow him to Park Lane, no one came forward. They were too weak for his 'form'. A hundred animated with his spirit might have made trouble, – but they were not to be found in *that* crowd. As the darkness came down over the column and the crowded square, and one departed back to warmth and shelter – while the meeting departed to cold and wretchedness, – one felt that all the raiding these dispirited, half-dead men would do would be harmless. Thirty well-fed policemen to the three thousand ill-nourished, shivering weaklings. That would be sufficient.

J. H. M. Abbott, 1905

THE IMMOVABLE POOR

It would seem that the district, as a whole, has gained little by the demolition of bad property within its borders, for the poorest and lowest cling most resolutely to the spot, merely shifting from one street to the next; and to some extent the area has certainly suffered from the additional crowding resulting from the clearances for railway or warehouse extension that have taken place in it. The process is going on from year to year. Site values rise, an advanced rent is demanded, and, by a paradox, the people leave in inverse proportion to their seeming ability to pay the advance – the

rich going first, the poorest last. The same thing has happened in the City of London. There the rich went first, the middle class followed, and the poor still linger in parts; in Southwark the rich have gone, the fairly comfortable are leaving, while the poor remain, and will remain till evicted. This general rule applies to a still larger area than that we are now considering, and when so applied has compensations which do not appear here. In other parts there is levelling up as well as levelling down; here it is not easy to trace the improvement which should follow when the poorest, whose houses are destroyed, move into the quarters abandoned by the better off.

Charles Booth, 1902

THE PRIZES OF PROSTITUTION

There is in this part a great concentration of evil living and low conditions of life that strikes the imagination and leads almost irresistibly to sensational statement. It contains a number of courts and small streets which for vice, poverty, and crowding, are unrivalled in London, and as an aggregate area of low life form perhaps the most serious blot to be found on the whole of our map. Of all the cases that come from the large district covered by the Southwark Police Court more than half are from this section. The inhabitants are not incomers from elsewhere, but mainly South Londoners born and bred. They are the dregs of this, not the scum of any other population.

Although greatly reduced and becoming rapidly less in quantity by demolitions, the palm for degradation was, at the time of our inquiry, still to be given to the group of old courts

Much slum clearance in London was carried out, before the local authorities took any interest in the subject, by railway builders and industrialists hungry for land. Most of Pitt's Place had been demolished to make room for the first Bankside Power Station, built for the City of London Electric Lighting Company in 1891. The surviving fragment, seen here in 1893, had only a temporary reprieve.

White Hind Alley, later Henslowe Passage, is seen here in 1896. It ran north from Pitt's Place to Bankside, along the wall of the old power station, which was eventually to engulf it.

lying between Red Cross Street and the Borough High Street. Revisiting them after an interval of ten years, I brought away the same black picture, the same depression of soul, as on the first occasion; the only relief being due to the destruction of some, and the only hope the prospective destruction of the rest. Those who live in these courts are neither all bad nor all poor, but to a great extent they are both; the men are waterside labourers and market porters and others of the lowest casual and loafing class, including thieves and the bullies who live on the earnings of prostitutes. Of this spot I have the following note written by one of my secretaries: 'Women with draggled skirts slouch by, their shawls on their heads. Undergrown men hang about. As I passed along three women stood gossiping on a doorstep; one of them was suckling a child openly with bare breasts. She showed no shyness. All were of the lowest type. Many evil faces, and a deformed boy with naked twisted leg completed the picture.' There is always a chance (say the police) of a salutation from some window by brickbat or a pail of slops, and it would be a black look out, they add, 'for anyone the worse for drink who might stumble in, or be brought in, at night. He would surely be robbed of everything and be lucky if he escaped unhurt.' Such opportunities are the prizes of prostitution here, and the economic justification of the bully,

This demonstration of scientific baby washing and dressing was given at Childeric Road School, New Cross, in 1908, only six years after the events described by Jack London. Self-defence did not make part of the syllabus.

for and with whom the woman lives. Into such quarters the police do not go unless they must, and then not singly: but it is right to add that for any sober, self-respecting passer by there is no likelihood of offence. Our own visits at night produced nothing more sensational than in the day.

Charles Booth, 1902

THE THING

'He is a good-looking man, with a mass of black hair, dark, expressive eyes, delicately chiselled nose and chin, and wavy, fair moustache.' This is the reporter's description of Frank Cavilla as he stood in court, this dreary month of September, 'dressed in a much worn grey suit, and wearing no collar.'

Frank Cavilla lived and worked as a house decorator in London. He is described as a good workman, a steady fellow, and not given to drink, while all his neighbours unite in testifying that he was a gentle and affectionate husband and father.

His wife, Hannah Cavilla, was a big, handsome, light-hearted woman. She saw to it that his children were sent neat and clean (the neighbours all remarked the fact), to the Childeric Road Board School. And so, with such a man, so blessed, working steadily and living temperately, all went well, and the goose hung high.

Then the thing happened. He worked for a Mr. Beck, builder, and lived in one of his master's houses in Trundley Road. Mr. Beck was thrown from his trap and killed. The thing was an unruly horse, and, as I say, it happened. Cavilla had to seek fresh employment and find another house.

This occurred eighteen months ago. For eighteen months he fought the big fight. He got rooms in a little house in Batavia Road, but could not make both ends meet. Steady work could not be obtained. He struggled manfully at casual employment of all sorts, his wife and four children starving before his eyes. He starved himself, and grew weak, and fell ill. This was three months ago, and then there was absolutely no food at all. They made no complaint, spoke no word; but poor folk know. The housewives of Batavia Road sent them food, but so respectable were the Cavillas that the food was sent anonymously, mysteriously, so as not to hurt their pride.

The thing had happened. He had fought, and starved, and suffered for eighteen months. He got up one September morning, early. He opened his pocket-knife. He cut the throat of his wife, Hannah Cavilla, aged thirty-three. He cut the throat of his first-born, Frank, aged twelve. He cut the throat of his son, Walter, aged eight. He cut the throat of his daughter, Nellie, aged four. He cut the throat of his youngest-born, Ernest, aged sixteen months. Then he watched beside the dead all day until the evening, when the police came, and he told them to put a penny in the slot of the gas-meter in order that they might have light to see.

Frank Cavilla stood in court, dressed in a much worn grey suit, and wearing no collar. He was a good-looking man, with a mass of black hair, dark, expressive eyes, delicately chiselled nose and chin, and wavy, fair moustache.

Jack London, 1903

In a traditional Guildhall scene, the members of the organising committee of the 1902 Lord Mayor's Feast prepare to divide the leftovers among the most deserving of the City's poor.

CITY CHARITIES

Scattered about the historic building are a number of tables, laden with pies, joints, and other good things left from the Lord Mayor's banquet on the previous evening. The remains of the feast have previously been divided by the pantrymen into as many portions as there are members of the committee which carries out the arrangements, usually twelve, and these gentlemen, duly aproned for the occasion, are now carving the pies and joints according to the number of the tickets they have given away. All being in readiness, the delighted recipients are each made happy with a substantial basketful of the capital fare. Some, you notice, get besides a portion of the world-famed turtle soup. These have invalids at home. But this epicurean delicacy is not always appreciated. The taste for it, like that for olives or tomatoes, must be acquired, and so the semi-liquid part of the gift sometimes descends hastily to the cat or dog.

Desmond Young, 1903

LADIES OF THE DAY

The lady collectors for 'Hospital Sunday' parade the streets once a year money-box in hand. Indeed, they pursue passers-by with the same insistence as ladies of another profession at night. Girls and young women in dainty costumes and respectable old ladies do their business with an almost appalling intensity. They are to be found at the corners of avenues, on the pathways, before public monuments, in front

The sirens of charity making another conquest on Hospital Saturday, 1893. Unless Mourey had misremembered, it would seem that the day was moved to Sunday in the following year.

The most grandiose result of the 'slumming' obsession with the East End was the building of the People's Palace in the Mile End Road. This large complex, designed by E.R. Robson, the chief architect of the School Board for London, was begun in the mid-1880s. The principal part, seen here in 1891, survives as Queen Mary College.

of banks, close to the Exchange, on the threshold of public-houses; truly their chase after charity makes them far more annoying than professional beggars. They strive to compel you with sweet voices full of promises, then they take you by the arm as they hold their money-box before you, until you are obliged to give in.

Gabriel Mourey, 1895

THE PALACE OF DELIGHT

The People's Palace has grown out of a legacy of £13,000 left by Mr. J. T. Barber Beaumont in 1841 to provide, in his own words, 'intellectual improvement and rational recreation and amusement for people living at the East End of London.' With the form which Mr. Beaumont's benevolent scheme finally assumed the late Sir Walter Besant had not a little to do, for it was largely due to the fascinating descriptions of a Palace of Delight for the people which are to be found in 'All Sorts and Conditions of Men' that there sprang up this admirable institution, which provides educational facilities for the toiling masses at the same time that it furnishes them with recreation and amusement. The People's Palace now forms the East London College, and includes a technical day school for 400 boys, a day college for older students, evening classes in general as well as technical subjects, and large engineering workshops. But it is much more than this. It comprises the Queen's Hall — so called because it was opened by Queen Victoria in 1887 — adorned with statues of the Queens of England placed between the double Corinthian columns that support the roof; a domed library, modelled on the reading-room of the British Museum, and opened in 1888; a swimming-bath, the gift of Lord Rosebery, opened in the same year; the Winter Garden, a glazed wing on the western side, presented by Lord Iveagh, and opened in 1892; and gymnasia and a school of art. These buildings, together with the technical school, were all designed by Mr. E. R. Robson, who has given to the structure a façade of no little dignity. In front of the Palace, which stands back from the road, is an elegant clock-and-fountain tower, reared by Mr. Herbert Stern in 1890 in memory of his father, Baron de Stern.

W. W. Hutchings, 1909

Chapter 10

IMPROVEMENTS

In London we call any act of destruction an Improvement. Despite the experience of two centuries the name has remained in use, a perseverance that testifies more highly to our self-confidence than to our discernment. One might have thought that the demolition of Nash's masterpiece, an act of vandalism known as the Regent Street Improvement, would have brought the term into disrepute, but apparently nothing can. In the late 1950s and early '60s the Park Lane Improvement put a motorway between Mayfair and Hyde Park and the St Giles's Circus Improvement gave us Centre Point.

Three of the most significant London road schemes, Holborn Viaduct, Charing Cross Road and Shaftesbury Avenue, were completed a little before 1887. After that date the only Improvement on the same scale was the long-debated one involving the construction of Kingsway and The Aldwych, and the destruction of a large number of ancient streets and buildings. Work on this epic scale was becoming prohibitively expensive, and since then only the chances of war have given scope for such sweeping changes.

Although grand schemes were becoming rarer, there were many smaller adjustments to the street pattern during these decades. Under the pressure of increasing traffic the London County Council and the Corporation of London were constantly seeking opportunities to widen roads and ease corners. Whitehall was transformed by the growth of bureaucracy, as the need for more offices led to the eviction of rich and poor alike from their mansions and hovels. There was plenty here to keep the planners happy.

They have always been wonderfully adept at exploiting the passing vagaries of architectural taste. An Australian visitor at the start of Edward VII's reign, in directing fellow tourists to the Temple Church (which turned his prose to gushing purple), advised them to 'pass by the two ugly churches of St Mary-le-Strand and St Clement Danes'. This was not a purely Antipodean judgement. The devoted Londoner William Pett Ridge declared with little regret that they would 'have to go', and in this climate of opinion the London County Council was fully prepared to demolish St Mary's as part of its Aldwych scheme. Only a testimonial from the architect's department that it was quite a good example of church building, for its date, prompted a change of heart. Fluctuations of taste have laid almost every London monument open to such attack at one time or another, as the destruction of Wren churches like St Olave's demonstrates. If all the plans filed away like time-bombs in the local government offices of London were to be implemented simultaneously there would scarcely be a fine building left standing in the capital.

Among the first and best buildings to appear in the Aldwych were the Waldorf Hotel, which opened in 1908, and the two matching theatres that flank it. In this early view, the near one is the Aldwych Theatre, and the far one the Waldorf, which was soon renamed the Strand. Note the vacant building plots in the foreground.

MITRED GOTHS AND VANDALS

Some years ago, having to review a book on the City churches in a newspaper, I ventured on a line of argument for which we have plenty of precedent. I did not keep a copy, nor am I perfectly sure of the expressions used, but, roughly speaking, the review commenced as follows: 'When the King of Italy wants money for a new ironclad, he adds to his resources by paying a visit to the Uffizzi. There he chooses a priceless Raphael and tears it from its frame, destroying it in the process. He is then able to obtain an appreciable sum towards his man-of-war by selling the space so gained to a photographer or a hairdresser.' This apothegm I ventured to apply, *mutato nomine*, to the Bishop of London. This is not the place to enlarge on the subject. Every now and then, generally in vacation time, a little note occurs in the ecclesiastical intelligence mentioning one of Wren's churches, pointing out its uselessness – want of congregation, generally, though any City church is at once filled by a competent incumbent – and insinuating that there is another church in the same street. This feeler will be recognized by anyone who reads the papers. It occurred in several places last September, and always heralds the same proposal. It is fully recognized now that only by a very extensive use of hyperbole, or, as statesmen put it, by much

terminological inexactitude, will the City parishioners be persuaded to 'tear down their Raphaels,' or destroy their Wren churches even to contribute to the Bishop's fund and build little eyesores in the suburbs. The fund suffers incalculably owing to the unpopularity caused by such a case as that of St Antholin, Watling Street. Here a beautiful tower which Wren had specially designed to set forth a contrast with the square Gothic tower of the next church, St Mary Aldermary, was condemned by means of a fiction and destroyed, to the irreparable loss of a great many precious things, including the credit for veracity of the episcopal committee.

I remember, in 1880, what an outcry was raised all over Europe because the new Khedive of Egypt allowed his grandmother to take some stones from a minor pyramid to be used in the building of a mosque at Cairo. Yet at that very time the people of a parish in the City of London gave permission to the Bishop to pull down the tower of All Hallows, Upper Thames Street, on the river front in every view. Very soon after, St Olave, Old Jewry (part of which was of thirteenth-century Gothic, by the way), to say nothing of St Antholin, which was worth more than many minor pyramids, was also razed to the ground.

William John Loftie, 1914

A mercifully rare opportunity to snap up a Wren church. This was St Olave, Old Jewry, shortly before the nave was demolished in 1888. The Korea Exchange Bank is now on the site. The tower survived to become part of an office in Ironmonger Lane.

A RUSH FOR THE SPOILS

It is no part of the writer's purpose to revive the rather unhappy memories of the negotiations, so to call them, between St. Bartholomew's and Christ's Hospitals, with a view to the enlargement of the former by the acquisition of a portion of our site. It will suffice to say that in the session of 1901 the Governors of St. Bartholomew's, desiring to purchase an acre and a half of the school site, and being unable to convince our Council that £117,000 was fair value for it, obtained an Act of Parliament in which there was a clause enjoining arbitration as the method by which the price should be settled. In the meantime, owing to the general idea that the beneficent work of St. Bartholomew's was being cramped for want of room and hindered by the possession of old-fashioned buildings, there arose a further movement for acquiring the whole of our site. In the end, it was decided to proceed to arbitration, the difficult post of divider and judge between two noble charities being accepted by Lord Balfour of Burleigh. He dealt with an area of an acre and one-third, about 67,680 superficial feet, and he awarded Christ's Hospital the very acceptable sum of £238,781. We may well subscribe to the philosophy of a medical journal, which remarked, 'Whichever gains by the transaction, the public benefits.'

Even before this there had been differences with the London County Council, who wanted 'the Garden' as an open space and our older buildings as a museum, and who, said their opponents, wanted still more a foothold in the City. But Parliament thought otherwise. St. Bartholomew's received its desired portion. We were left in possession of the rest, that it might be disposed of to the best advantage. So it has happened, and for the present it continues to be the case, that a portion of our old home stands where it did. The Grammar School and the 'Mathemat' with 'Fourteens', 'Fifteens', and 'Sixteens' remain outwardly as they were. They have become commodious nurses' quarters, and, until an arrogant ferro-concrete town, if I may borrow from Mr. E. V. Lucas, arose between the vicarage and those haunts of Dr. Jacob's grammars, we still had the feeling that something yet remained of the old familiar life. The light that gleams nightly from Fifteens, where I was a junior Grecian, is, I think, electric. Other times, other illuminants. But it is a comfort as long as it lasts.

A word or two as to the southern portion of our site. The intention of the Governing Body was to develop it and live happily upon the ground-rents. A street was to have bisected it from east to west, and all was in train for what might or might not have been a profitable enterprise, and would in any case have been an anxious one, when His Majesty's Government stepped in one morning in December, 1903, and claimed it for the purposes of a new distributing centre for the ever-increasing correspondence of the Empire. It was hoped by many of us, and even now it is hard to see why the hope could not have been realised, that the Post Office might have spared the Hospital a corner in these ancient acres for the erection of a Counting-House. But we were not even given the alternatives of all or nothing; it must be all, absolutely all. Financially the result has been more than consolatory. No anxiety as to whether we should find a

The great hall at Christ's Hospital was famous for its rats, and the frames of the huge historical paintings on its walls were their favourite playground. By 1902 the rats had probably deserted, but removing the pictures for their journey to the new school at Horsham was still no light task.

market for the plots on the new estate; no qualms about the premises falling empty, or the neighbourhood going out of fashion. Only the labour, such as it is, of drawing on Government for £23,000 a year in perpetuity.

E. H. Pearce, 1908

MASSIVE SPLENDOUR

What, one imagines, would modern London have been had Inigo Jones's plan found fruition, and the whole of Whitehall, from Westminster to the Banqueting House, been given up to his palatial splendours? That the present Buckingham Palace is but a poor substitute for such imagined magnificence is certain, and the loss of Inigo's fine Palladian river-frontage is perhaps hardly atoned for by the terrace of our modern Houses of Parliament; yet these, too, are beautiful, and Whitehall has not lost its palatial air; for its wide and still widening streets, its spacious and imposing Government Offices, still serve to keep up the illusion, and, at any rate, the state of royalty. Already one of the handsomest streets in London, its buildings are being yet further improved, and a new War Office of vast proportions is rising slowly on the long-vacant plot of ground where, it was said, three hundred different kinds of wild flowers lately grew, whose yellow and pink blossoms used to wave temptingly before the eyes of travellers on omnibus-tops. . . . Now, never more will flowers grow there; no longer will the picturesque, green-gabled roofs of 'Whitehall Court' look across to the fleckered sunlight of the Admiralty and the Horse Guards. Instead, palatial buildings, something after the Palladian manner of Inigo Jones's imagined Whitehall Palace, will form a noble street, in a more or less continuous line of massive splendour; a road of palaces, to be further dignified by the erection of new and spacious Government Offices, near the Abbey, on the line of the destroyed and obstructive King Street. When all the Whitehall improvements are carried out, the dignity and beauty of London will gain immensely, and the view down the long street of palaces, – the Abbey, unobstructed by intervening buildings, shining like a star at its Parliament Street end, – will be among the very finest sights in the metropolis.

Mrs. E. T. Cook, 1902

CONTEMPT OF COURTS

I admire the exterior of the Law Courts. I am told I ought not to do so, and that is not the right thing to admire any part of the structure, outside or inside. But I cannot help myself – I cannot get over my invincible ignorance, and I stop every now and then in front of the Courts and look on them with admiration. I also admire the long, narrow hall. But my admiration comes to a stop there. Anything meaner, more uncomfortable, more ugly than the various little courts themselves, was never put together by the perverted ingenuity of man. It would be hard to exaggerate the utterly paradoxical character of these remarkable courts. They are

The photographer who snapped J.M. Brydon's new Local Government Board offices (below) c. 1910 chose the same vantage point as the artist who sketched the demolition of King Street and the west side of Parliament Street in 1898. Other ancient places that vanished for the sake of this bureaucratic triumph were Gardener's Row and Boar's Head Yard. The old premises of the Local Government Board, part of Gilbert Scott's great block of the 1860s and '70s (the Foreign Office, etc.) are seen on the right of both pictures.

too small; they are too large; they are too dark; they are too glaring; they are too hot; they are too cold; it is impossible to hear what a witness is saying, and yet each court is like a whispering gallery to send along the muttered gossip of some idle spectator. The draughts that howl through these rooms make one fancy he is in the Cave of Æolus. The great curtains which are hung at the doors are so arranged that they involve the hapless stranger trying to enter as if he were being rolled in a huge blanket. If you are seated securely in the court it is interesting to watch the struggles of this hapless stranger. You see his form bulging here and there through the thick drapery in which he has ignorantly invested himself. He thought he had nothing to do but to draw the curtain aside and go in: he did draw the curtain aside, but it took him into its folds and rolled itself round and round him, and look how he is struggling rightfully to be free! He plunges this way, and the curtain plunges with him; that way, and the curtain takes a new twist about him. At last he emerges, wrathful, shameful, his face red and glowing, and his hat – his poor hat,

*The Royal Courts of Justice,
better known as the Law Courts,
began the great alteration of the
Strand that ended with the
Aldwych. They took more than a
decade to build (1871–82) and
not only killed their designer,
G.E. Street, but proved 'the
death-knell of the old-fashioned
scholarly Gothic'.*

which he has had to carry in his hand through the thick of
the fight! He knows that his face is dirty as well as red, for the
curtain has clung to his bewildered countenance, and he is
not without a fear that my Lord on the bench may have seen
him, and may have thought he was doing it all for the fun of
the thing, and perhaps may commit him for contempt of
court. Contempt of court indeed! Who is there that could
avoid feeling a contempt for that court?

Justin MacCarthy, 1893

A STRAND IN BOHEMIA

The busy, crowded Strand has, until the last widening and
improvements spoilt its fun, been the rendezvous of the
members of *the* profession and others connected with the stage.
When I first made its acquaintance London's Bohemia consisted
of a ramshackle, picturesque, and historically interesting jumble
of famous old streets, narrow passages, 'inns', square taverns, and
publishing shops. In this interesting quarter jostled together vice
and virtue, intellect and ignorance, poverty and opulence.

*Among the many buildings
demolished to make room for the
Aldwych were nos. 263 to 266
The Strand, seen here from
St Clement Danes Church in
1901. Clement's Lane is on the
right, and the narrow entrance to
Wych Street on the left.*

In this Alsatia dwelt 'characters' both eccentric and clever, and, if not inspiring, they were at least artistic. The very pavements reeked with tobacco from the calumets of semi-savages, combined with the onions accompanying the chops and steaks which were carried from the cook-shop to the office of the wealthy banker or the establishment of the well-to-do tradesman.

All these odoriferous rookeries have been razed to the ground, and upon their site have arisen stately and imposing edifices in which are to be found the offices of the Marconi Company, colonial agencies, banks, etc., together with palatial newspaper and other offices. In such an environment it is impossible that Bohemianism could ever exist. It would be a gross anachronism. As a matter of fact the death of Bohemianism is really due more to the genius of the architect than to any vagaries of fashion or fortune.

Harry Furniss, 1919

SCATHING JOKE AND REPARTEE

You have perhaps reached Walker's Court and Berwick Street, the brightest spot surely in all London on a Saturday night, or you are in Little Earl Street, one of the spokes of the Seven Dials wheel, or it may be that you have tumbled on the remains of old Clare Market. The people crowd the streets, along which no vehicle dreams of passing, chatting with each other, chaffering with the sellers, buying what they want or looking on while others buy. The air is bright with flaring lights and resonant with voices. The street is occupied by a double line of "costers'" barrows and three slowly flowing streams of passers-by, one on each sidewalk, in the narrow space left between the wares pushed forward by the shops and those displayed on the barrows; a space so restricted and so fully occupied by sellers and buyers that no one else (unless indeed he be a student of such doings) will attempt the passage; while in the wider space between barrow and barrow in the centre of the street those stroll along who are not immediately concerned in the traffic.

The noisiest sellers are those who sell meat. They shout to the general 'buy, buy, *buy*, BUY, BUY,' repeated rapidly with a sharpening of the sound on each repetition of the word till the last rings like blow of hammer upon steel. But to the particular they address soft words – 'Now, my dear, what can I do for you?' – or confidential recommendation of some particular bit of meat. Where there is one butcher's shop another is always close by, and between-whiles the men will shout loud chaff to their rival over the way, with seemingly an inexhaustible supply of scathing joke and repartee, taken and given with perfect geniality in the very best cockney spirit, suggesting somewhat the old days of 'Chepe' with frolicsome apprentices crying 'what d'ye lack?'

Charles Booth, 1889

JAMES ANDERSON, TRAGEDIAN

Shortly after seeing him as Antony, I recollect passing along Old Wych Street, in the Strand, and observing him standing with his back to a shop door, gazing intently at an oil painting which was high up in the window of a second-hand shop opposite to him. I recalled this little incident to him years afterwards in the smoking-room of the Garrick Club. Taking me into another room, he showed me, framed, that very portrait I saw him looking at years before – it was a portrait of himself in *Coriolanus*.

Clare Market, one of the better-known victims of the Aldwych/Kingsway clearances, specialised in meat and other foodstuffs, but its most notorious products were crime and vice. It is shown here in 1891.

With their curious belief that a human need could be eradicated along with the place in which it was satisfied, most Victorians were glad to see the end of Wych Street and Holywell Street, not only because they were so picturesque, but because this was the centre of the trade in erotic books. Wych Street, seen here in the 1890s, was soon to disappear beneath the Aldwych.

When he was a younger actor and the rage of London, playing Coriolanus, a young unknown artist begged Anderson to sit for his portrait in character, as it would be a good advertisement for the young artist. Anderson never saw the painting or the artist again until, as an old man, he spied it hanging up in the second-hand shop. 'I wondered was it a portrait of myself, so I went to the other side of the street to have a good look at it. There was no mistaking it, my boy; it was Jimmy Anderson's neck. There is not another man in the world with so long a neck as mine.'

Harry Furniss, 1919

PROGRESSIVE DEGRADATION

The dark side of the district lies about Drury Lane. From Seven Dials going east the tone gets lower and lower till we reach that black patch consisting of Macklin Street, Shelton Street, Parker Street. Shelton Street has now been demolished, and parts of the other two are destroyed or scheduled for destruction. The change proceeds so fast that what was already is not, and much of what still is, will perhaps no longer be before these lines are in print. From this spot, through Great Wild Street and Vere Street, past old Clare Market to the Law Courts, we have at any rate nothing worse to encounter, but it is to be feared that the clearances made and making are being, and will be, paid for by the further degradation of the district towards the Strand. They must then in their turn be scheduled and pulled down.

Eastward of Seven Dials lie many groups of common lodging-houses. In some live sandwich-men, loafers, and the most casual of casual labourers; other houses are the resort of ticket-of-leave men, and those who have been, or sooner or later will become, acquainted with prison life. Others accommodate the lowest of women, and some again provide double accommodation.

Charles Booth, 1902

THE PALIMPSEST

It has been given to the Londoner of to-day to witness the greatest evisceration of the town that has been known since the Fire of 1666. A little more than a dozen years ago the Clare Market region was a humming neighbourhood, full of race and tradition, a secret labyrinth without omnibuses or newsboys. All the traditions of piecemeal change, casualness, and compromise which have made London picturesque were flouted in the Kingsway and Aldwych scheme. The surfaces of the new arteries are now the palimpsest of a populous quarter, of which St Mary's and St Clement's churches are the gracious relics.

One of the most interesting vestiges – not finally destroyed until this year – was the old horseshoe archway on the west side of Lincoln's Inn Fields leading into what was yesterday Sardinia Street. Twenty years ago you passed through it from the desolate exclusiveness of Lincoln's Inn Fields (the garden was not opened to the public till 1895), into the populous dirt and colour of the whole Clare Market region; either way that squat and grudging archway led from one London world to another.

Wilfred Whitten, 1913

A DRASTIC CLEARANCE

From 1836 onwards schemes were framed from time to time which had for their objects the widening of the Strand between its two churches, and the construction of an arterial street between the Strand and Holborn, but when the London County Council succeeded the Metropolitan Board of Works, in 1889, it found the task still unattempted. Nor need the delay be regretted, for the probability is that, had the enterprise been undertaken earlier, it would not have been carried out on so large a scale. Not only have we now a crescent stretching from Wellington Street on the west to St. Clement's on the east, of a uniform breadth of a hundred feet, with a spacious 'island' in half-moon form between it and the Strand, and a thoroughfare of the same noble breadth running from it to Holborn, but the Clare Market and other insanitary areas have been cleared. Altogether some twenty-eight acres of property were dealt with, and near seven thousand persons were dispossessed of their dwellings, of whom over six thousand were re-housed, some on the cleared area, but the greater number at Millbank and elsewhere. To the lover of old London such a drastic clearance as this cannot but bring feelings of regret, but it must

Vere Street lay directly on the route of Kingsway, and did not survive even as a name. This photograph was taken in 1904. By 1905 only the Board School was still standing – it is on the left of the photograph on page 120 – and even that soon made way for the London Opera House.

be admitted that the changes were inevitable, and that the compensations are not inconsiderable.

It was in 1898 that the scheme was finally adopted by the Council. But two years before this a beginning had been made with it by the annihilation of the Holywell Street block of houses, stretching between the churches of St. Clement Danes and St. Mary-le-Strand. In 1897 a clean sweep was made of the alleys and

The old Sardinia Street, seen here in 1902, was also extinguished by the relentless march of Kingsway. Its modern successor is in a different position. The archway into the contrasting world of Lincoln's Inn Fields lay around the corner.

The desolation from which Kingsway was born. In 1905 this was the view south towards the Aldwych from the Kemble Street area. Vere Street Board School (see page 119) is on the left, and the tower of St Mary-le-Strand in the distance.

courts between Clare Market and Drury Lane, and in the same year Southampton Row, at Holborn, was broadened. The complete thoroughfare, street and crescent, from the junction of Southampton Row and Theobald's Road to the Strand, is just over three-quarters of a mile in length (4,200 feet), and except for a short distance in Southampton Row, where it is 80 feet wide, its breadth is a hundred feet. It was opened on the 18th of October, 1905.

W. W. Hutchings, 1909

FEARFUL OMENS

The Foreign Office of the Salvation Army tells us that the Army is already established in twenty-seven countries, and before long will be in evidence in several others. Some idea of the widespread nature of the great work begun by the late 'General' Booth may be gained from the facts that representatives of some fifty peoples took part in the recent procession of delegates to the Salvation Army's 'Congress of

The island site between the Aldwych and the Strand attracted few permanent buildings until after 1918, but various temporary structures, mostly evangelical, rose and fell. On the Strand side, just east of St Mary's, the Salvation Army Fort made several appearances, in 1904 for example, and here in 1914, when it accommodated the International Christian Congress.

The car had ousted the horse when this photograph of Westminster Bridge was taken, c. 1913. Across the river can be seen, on the left, the vacant site on which County Hall was about to rise, and on the right the splendid pavilions of St Thomas's Hospital. A foreign visitor gazing across the river from the terrace of the House of Commons once asked her host, 'Are these the palaces of your nobility?'

Nations', and that thirty-five languages or dialects are being spoken at that Congress. At a meeting held the other day, an ingenious method of interpretation was used. Interpreters, scattered here and there among the audience, re-told the story of the speaker in various tongues. Each of them carried a box-telephone, to which were attached a number of receivers, through which foreign delegates heard the address in their own languages. The Congress, which is being attended by about 2100 delegates, began on June 11 and will end on the 26th, with a demonstration in the Albert Hall. The temporary building in the Strand at the foot of Kingsway (to be pulled down after a fortnight's use) holds 5000 people, and here most of the business of the Congress has been conducted. The picturesque costumes of the Overseas delegates have attracted much interest. Members of the Salvation Army who are reservists of the German Army wear their military uniforms while on parade with the religious organisation. A sad note is touched by the thought that over a hundred Salvationists on their way to the Congress lost their lives in the 'Empress of India' disaster.

'Illustrated London News', 1914

BUILT ON OSIERS

Northwards from the Albert Embankment runs the Belvedere Road, and the ground lying between the southern part of this street and the river was formerly styled the Pedlar's Acre. In the fifteenth and sixteenth century it was known as Church Osiers, from a large osier bed. The ground was at some period bequeathed to the parish, but no proof has been found of the tradition that it was the dying gift of a pedlar who imposed the condition that he and his dog were to be perpetually commemorated in painted glass in the parish church. In Belvedere Road was the establishment of the Works Department of the London County Council,

until in 1909 it was broken up, and it is here that ground has been acquired for the new County Hall, which is to be reared, at a cost of about a million and three-quarters, from the designs of that brilliant young architect, Mr. Ralph Knott.

W. W. Hutchings, 1909

A HOLLOW SHAM

Once outside the Tower precincts, all is changed, and you are, again, in the bustle and the din of modern London. 'Great Tower Hill', on the rising ground north of the Tower, and close to Mark Lane Station, is hardly an idyllic spot, or one at

Trinity Square in 1912, just before all these buildings were demolished to make way for the headquarters of the Port of London Authority. Catherine Court (on the left), which led to Seething Lane, was also completely destroyed.

Robinson and Cleaver of Belfast, the linendrapers, rebuilt most of their shop at 156 to 169 Regent Street in 1910. It was part of the creeping destruction of Nash's great work that became inevitable after Norman Shaw's design for the Piccadilly Hotel was allowed to go ahead in 1905.

all suitable to meditation, being generally much invaded by the shouts of draymen and the rumble of van wheels. Close by, in Trinity Square gardens, marked by a stone, is the spot which for some centuries shared with 'Tyburn' the honour, or dishonour, of being the public execution place.

Trinity Square has still a pleasant, old-fashioned air of seclusion; although all around and about it are grimy lanes and warehouses, suggesting the close proximity of wharves and docks. Yet Trinity Square, like Charterhouse Square, is no longer residential; the look of 'home', of comfortable family life, about its sober brick houses, is merely a hollow sham; they are mainly offices.

Mrs. E. T. Cook, 1902

A NOBLE THOROUGHFARE

The disappearance of the pillars, of which some faint traces may yet be visible where Air Street intersects the Quadrant, was regarded by foreigners as an almost phenomenal illustration of the stupid indifference of Londoners to the handsomeness of their own Metropolis. For at least twenty years the Regent's Quadrant had been looked upon by the French as one of the few really comely architectural adornments of London. Views of the Quadrant were often engraved in books of English travel written by French, German, and even Italian and Spanish sojourners in our midst; and I have before me a sheet of French note-paper full fifty years old, the top of which bears a tastefully engraved vignette of the Quadrant, to which the Continental artist has

given the widely embracing and somewhat arrogant title of 'La Ville de Londres'.

I daresay that country cousins still think this part of Regent Street very grandiose, and their admiration may be shared by our American visitors; and, I should say, to the majority of competent judges of architectural effect, the Quadrant, shorn of its colonnade, presents only the aspect of two very bald and monotonous façades; the only curiosity connected with which, is that they are built on a curve forming the fourth of a circle.

George Augustus Sala, 1894

A SIGN OF THE TIMES

Lovers of old London, whether of the City or the suburbs, are glad to see a revival of taste everywhere. That antiquity and picturesqueness go hand in hand is often true, but it is also true that of things new now but few will rank as worthy to survive and become picturesque in their turn. It is for this reason that we must lament the extensive use of stucco in a past generation, and especially at a time when good design was to be had in a hundred directions. There would be no more beautiful building and none more happy in its situation than the Insurance Office at the foot of the Quadrant, if it could be correctly described as a building and not a mere plaster model or mould. It is a sign of the times, and a happy one, that the Quadrant is to be rebuilt in stone.

William John Loftie, 1914

THE END

Britain's declaration of war on Germany being proclaimed from the steps of the Royal Exchange on 5 August 1914.

INDEX